REVISE EDEXCEL
FUNCTIONAL SKILLS LEVEL 2

English

REVISION GUIDE

Series Consultant: Harry Smith

Author: Julie Hughes

A note from the publisher

In order to ensure that this resource offers high-quality support for the associated Pearson qualification, it has been through a review process by the awarding body. This process confirms that this resource fully covers the teaching and learning content of the specification or part of a specification at which it is aimed. It also confirms that it demonstrates an appropriate balance between the development of subject skills, knowledge and understanding, in addition to preparation for assessment.

Endorsement does not cover any guidance on assessment activities or processes (e.g. practice questions or advice on how to answer assessment questions), included in the resource nor does it prescribe any particular approach to the teaching or delivery of a related course.

While the publishers have made every attempt to ensure that advice on the qualification and its assessment is accurate, the official specification and associated assessment guidance materials are the only authoritative source of information and should always be referred to for definitive guidance.

Pearson examiners have not contributed to any sections in this resource relevant to examination papers for which they have responsibility.

Examiners will not use endorsed resources as a source of material for any assessment set by Pearson.

Endorsement of a resource does not mean that the resource is required to achieve this Pearson qualification, nor does it mean that it is the only suitable material available to support the qualification, and any resource lists produced by the awarding body shall include this and other appropriate resources.

THE REVISE SERIES
For the full range of Pearson revision titles, visit:
www.pearsonschools.co.uk/revise

Contents

1-to-1
page match with the Level 2 Revision Workbook
ISBN 978 1 292 14579 2

A small bit of small print

Edexcel publishes Sample Assessment Material and the Specification on its website. This is the official content and this book should be used in conjunction with it. The questions in Now try this have been written to help you practise every topic in the book. Remember: the real exam questions may not look like this.

Your reading and writing tests

To do well in your Functional Skills English qualification, you will need to prepare for your reading and writing tests.

Your reading test

You will have **60 minutes** to gain a total of **30 marks** in the reading test.

 Read all the questions.

 Read the three texts.

} (15 minutes)

 Answer all the questions. (40 minutes)

 Check your answers. (5 minutes)

Planning your time

Planning your time during the test is very important. Practise planning your time when you answer practice questions in this book.

Spend the first 15 minutes of your test familiarising yourself with the questions and the texts.

1 **Read the questions** to work out what you need to look for when you read the texts.

2 **Skim read the texts** to find the main ideas.

3 **Underline** any information you will need in your answers.

Your writing test

You will have **60 minutes** to gain a total of **30 marks** in the writing test. Each writing task will be worth **15 marks**.

 Read the task and any information provided.

 Produce a brief plan.

 Write a detailed answer.

 Check your work.

Checking your work

Always read your work through when you have finished writing. You should aim to spend two minutes checking that your answers are complete and correct.

 When you have finished reading each task, write a brief plan for your answer, including:

• your main ideas

• notes on the audience, purpose and format.

Getting it right

Divide your time evenly between the two tasks. Leave yourself plenty of time for the second task so that you aren't rushing your answer.

Now try this

1 What should you look for when you skim read the texts in the reading test?

2 How much time should you spend on each writing task?

3 What should you do when you have finished writing your answers?

Online tools 1

If you are completing the Functional Skills tests online, you will need to understand how the test works.

Before you start your online test read the instructions about how to use the test.

- Make sure you know what all the icons do.
- Make sure you can read the test clearly and easily.

Useful icons

You can click this **Time** icon to find out how much time you have left in your test. The time will appear in the bottom left-hand corner.

The timer does not stop when you click on the Help icon. Make sure you know how to use the test before you start. You will be reminded when you have 15 minutes left, and again when you have 5 minutes left in the test.

Time   Help   Review   Flag   Previous   Next   Exhibit   Translation   Quit   Status

You can click this **Help** icon if you want a demonstration of how the online test buttons work.

The **Previous** and **Next** icons move you from question to question.

Be very careful with the **Quit** icon. If you click on it and then select 'Yes', you will not be able to return to the test even if you haven't finished!

Changing the test settings

Click the ➕ icon in the bottom left-hand corner of the screen to open the Settings box.

Use the **colour reset** icon and the **zoom reset** icon to go back to the original test screen.

Click the **arrows** to move around the page when you are zoomed in.

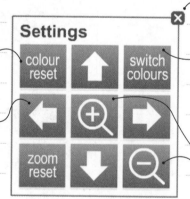

Settings

colour reset / switch colours / zoom reset

Click this **cross** to close the Settings box.

Click the **switch colours** icon to change the colour of the test to make it easier to read.

Click the **magnifying glass** icons to zoom in and out of the test.

Now try this

1 How do you find out how much time is left?
2 What can you do if you can't read the test clearly?

Online tools 2

There are useful tools on the online test that can help you plan your answers and your time.

The notepad tool

You can make notes to help you to remember key information and plan your answer.

The notepad tool takes you to a screen where you can:

- underline questions
- underline words and phrases in the reading texts
- make a plan for answering your writing tasks.

Click on this icon to open the notepad. Anything you type in this box will **not** be marked.

This icon will let you underline key words in the texts or questions. Make sure the shaded box covers the text you want to underline.

Click one of these icons to choose a colour for your notes. Choose a colour that is different from the text, so that you can see it clearly when writing your answers.

This icon clears everything in the notepad and all of your underlining. Make sure you don't press Clear All before you have finished and checked your work.

Formatting text

In the writing test, you can change the font and the presentation of text for emphasis.

> Go to pages 37 and 38 to read more about writing test skills and questions.

Flagging tricky questions

✓ Flag — If you are unsure how to answer a question, **flag** it and move on to the next question. Click this Flag icon so that you can come back to the question later.

Review — Before you check your answers, go back to any questions you have flagged. You can **review** them by clicking the Review icon.

Now try this

1 What **three** things can you use the notepad tool for?
2 What should you do if you are struggling to answer a question?

Reading texts

For your reading test, you will be asked to read three texts, all about the same real-world topic. You will be tested on how well you read and understand these texts.

Types of text

You could be asked to read any of the following types of text:

- advertisements
- blogs
- leaflets
- manuals
- transcripts.
- articles
- web comments
- letters
- text books

Identifying important features

In the test you should read all three texts carefully and identify the following:

- the main ideas
- the purpose
- the audience
- key information
- point of view, implicit meaning and bias.

This text is an advertisement. Advertisements can have several different **purposes**, including to inform and to persuade.

Look for clues in the text to work out who the **audience** is. Some audiences are more specific than others.

Text I

HOMELESS HAVEN

Homeless Haven provides food, housing, support and friendship for the homeless across the UK. We transform the lives of vulnerable people, by providing somewhere safe and comfortable to stay and by helping them get back on their feet.

Why should you volunteer?

Volunteering allows you to give something back to your community and help people who are less fortunate than you. Many of our clients are under 25, so it's a good opportunity to work with young people and help them secure a brighter future. ...

How can you volunteer?

We are looking for volunteers who are able to commit at least a day per week. If this applies to you, come and see us to find out how you can become part of our team and make a difference. We are open 24/7.

Headings can give you an idea of what the **theme** of a text is. Further reading will reveal the **main ideas** and **key information**.

When you read the three texts, remember to think about how the points of view differ. **Bias** is usually implied, rather than written explicitly. Look for clues in the text to inform you about the writer's opinion of the topic.

Now try this

1 Identify **five** features you should look for when reading a text.
2 Can a text be suitable for more than one audience?

Skimming for details

Skim reading a text helps you to locate key information and identify main ideas quickly.

Focusing your reading

When you skim read a text you should focus on key parts, such as:

- titles or headings
- the first sentence of each paragraph
- the last sentence of each paragraph
- numbers
- bullet points.

Skim reading tips

Skim reading is an important skill that you should learn and practise before your reading test.

To skim read effectively you need to:

- read the questions first so you have an idea of what you are looking for
- focus your reading on key parts of the text: you don't need to read every word when you are skim reading
- underline key words and phrases as you skim the text.

Getting it right

In the test you should read the whole text carefully, not just the title or heading.

The title, or heading, will usually give you a clue about the main idea of a text. Here, it suggests that the article is about the internet.

Bullet points or numbered lists may have sub-headings. Skim reading these will give you an idea of their topic focus.

Text B

WHO'S THE SLAVE? MASTERING THE ONLINE WORLD

With so much technology at our fingertips these days, it is easier than ever to waste hours watching funny videos of cats. Many people feel they have become slaves to their devices, checking their messages, reading the news and flicking through social media throughout the day for fear of missing out.

So, how do we use technology wisely? How do we become masters of the online world, rather than being its servants? Here are five top tips:

1. **Use it to save money** Many retailers post offers and vouchers on social networking sites, so 'Like' your favourite shops to stay up to date with the best deals. You can also cut down on your phone bill by messaging your friends through social media instead of using texts and phone calls.

The first sentence of each paragraph often gives you important information. Here, it tells you what the article is likely to be about and suggests that the writer's point of view is that we all waste time online.

The first sentence of the second paragraph suggests the purpose of the text is going to be to give advice.

Now try this

1 List **two** key places to skim for information in a text.
2 Why is it a good idea to read the questions before skim reading the text?

Underlining

In your reading test, underlining and circling key words and phrases can help you to access important information quickly and easily.

Underlining important information

Your annotations should be clear and simple. Only underline key words:

- commands
- direct address, e.g. 'you'
- facts and figures
- descriptive words
- literary devices
- emotive language.

> **literary device** *noun*
>
> a technique used by writers to produce a specific effect
>
> *Examples:* alliteration, analogy, cliché, hyperbole

Before you start underlining a text, you should do the following so that you can focus your reading.

- Read the questions.
- Pick out the key words in each question so that you know what to look out for in the text.
- Skim read the text to find the main ideas.

6 Your friend doesn't realise how serious the homelessness situation is for young people.

Using Text H, <u>advise</u> your friend on the <u>seriousness</u> of the homelessness situation for young people.

(2 marks)

Looking for key information

The key words in question 6 are 'advise' and 'seriousness'. To advise your friend about the seriousness of the homelessness situation, you need to find descriptive language, facts and figures in Text H to help.

The phrase 'wildly inaccurate' suggests that this writer believes that the situation is worse than people think.

'Over three times' also links to the situation being worse than expected.

The word 'crisis' emphasises the seriousness of the situation.

The last sentence suggests that statistics are wrong and the situation may be more serious than it seems.

Text H

MISERY RISES FOR THE YOUNG

Government figures for the number of young people who are homeless <u>are wildly inaccurate</u>, according to research undertaken by a leading university.

The survey suggests that over 85,000 16- to 25-year-olds were homeless in 2014. This is <u>over three times</u> the number stated in the Government's official figures. The research calls the levels of homelessness <u>'a crisis'</u>, particularly as many young people are resorting to begging in order to feed themselves. It also claims that the situation may be even worse than the figures suggest, as they <u>do not include those who are temporarily housed in shelters.</u>

Now try this

Re-read question 6 above, then read the whole of Text H on page 83. Annotate **three** parts of the text that would help you to answer the question.

Types of question

In the test, you should read each question carefully to make sure you know exactly what you are being asked to do.

Multiple choice questions

For multiple choice questions, you will be asked to select **one** correct answer from a choice of **four** options.

Read all the options carefully. Some multiple choice options sound similar or start with the same words or phrases.

Only one answer is needed for this question, as it is worth only one mark.

If you want to change your answer, cross out what you have written and write your new answer.

> **1** According to Text E, the writer believes that:
>
> **A** people realise how much fuel they waste ☐
>
> **B** people are not wasting fuel in their homes ☐
>
> **C** people know how much fuel they use ☐
>
> **D** people are not aware that fuel waste is a problem ☐
>
> (1 mark)

Short response questions

Short response questions can be worth anywhere between one and five marks. You should:

- read the instructions carefully
- think about what the question is asking you to do
- work out what you need to include in your answer and how long it needs to be
- if you are asked to use more than one text in your answer, mention the names of the texts to make sure it is clear which one you are talking about.

Getting it right

All your answers must use information from the text. Even if you know something about the topic, you will not get marks if you use information that is not in the texts provided.

Providing evidence

You could be asked to provide an example from the text to support your answer. You should make sure you give specific examples, relating to any of the following:

- content
- language
- layout.

You can use an exact quotation or you can paraphrase the text (put it into your own words) to support your answer.

> **2** Explain one way the writer of Text E tries to convince the reader that they should not use so much fuel.
>
> Give an example to support your answer.
>
> ....
>
> ....
>
> (2 marks)

Now try this

1 Why should you not include information in your answer that is not in the text?

2 Name **three** important things you should identify to fully understand a short response question.

Reading test skills

In the test you will need to demonstrate that you are able to:

- identify relevant information
- analyse content, language and layout
- summarise texts.

Selecting and using information

The reading test questions test your ability to fully understand a text by instructing you to select and use relevant information from the text.

For the test-style question on the right, you would need to do the following:

1. Skim read all three texts to decide which is the most relevant and least biased.

2. Read the text carefully to find an example to justify your choice.

3. Write your answer, including the name of the text, why it is most useful and an example from the text to support your reason.

> **11** You are preparing a talk about the link between homelessness and family breakdown.
>
> Which text is the **most** useful when preparing your talk?
>
> Give **one** reason for your choice and **one** example to support your answer.
>
> **(3 marks)**

Analysing more than one text

For some questions, you will need to draw out information from more than one text.

Here, you are asked to use both Text B and Text C. It is vital that you use the correct texts for questions like this one.

The key words in the question are 'benefits' and 'social networking'.

The question is worth 5 marks, so you should give a detailed answer. To do well in this type of question, you need to choose relevant information from both texts and link them to the audience's needs.

> **8** Your friend does not believe that social networking sites have any benefits.
>
> Using <u>Texts B and C</u>, advise your friend on the <u>benefits</u> of using <u>social networking</u> sites.
>
> ....
>
> ....
>
> ....
>
> **(5 marks)**

Summarising ideas

For some questions, you will need to summarise the main ideas of the text in a clear, concise way.

For this test-style question, you should read each text carefully and work out the main difference or differences in ideas.

For each difference, you will need to give an example from each text to back up your idea. You will probably need to paraphrase it, but it must come from the text.

> **10** Use <u>Text G and Text H</u> to answer this question.
>
> Explain how these texts have different ideas about arresting people for begging.
>
> Give <u>examples</u> from both texts to support your answer.
>
> **(5 marks)**

Now try this

Why is it important to read each question carefully before giving your answer?

Analysing texts

You need to demonstrate that you are able to analyse language and layout in texts to determine who the audience is, what the purpose is and what the point of view of the writer is.

Understanding the purpose

You will need to understand the aim of a text, and explain how the author uses language techniques to achieve it.

For this type of question you will need to identify different language techniques.

This longer question is worth four marks, so you will need to give quotations **and** explain how they are convincing.

> **5** In Text E, which of the following is an example of direct address:
>
> **A** 'Teenagers are often the worst offenders here' ☐
>
> **B** 'Fuel waste is a massive problem in the UK.' ☐
>
> **C** 'half the rooms in your house could be sitting empty' ☐
>
> **D** 'government grants are available to help' ☐
>
> **(1 mark)**

> **7** Identify **two** methods the writer of Text C uses to convince the reader that children benefit from spending time online.
>
> Give an example to support your answer.
>
> **(4 marks)**

Identifying the point of view

You could be asked to explain the writer's point of view or bias about a topic.

You may also need to identify what is implied by a text. This is the meaning hidden behind the author's words but not stated directly.

> **2** In Text G, what do the following quotations suggest about the writer's view of people who beg for money?
>
> **(2 marks)**

> **3** What does 'Wrong. Fuel waste is a massive problem in the UK.' imply about people's understanding of fuel waste?
>
> **(1 mark)**

Understanding the audience

You need to understand who a text is intended for, and how it can help them.

In this question, you need to identify the important facts in an informative piece of writing.

> **8** Your friend does not realise how serious fuel wastage in the UK is.
>
> Using Texts D and F, explain the seriousness of the situation.
>
> **(4 marks)**

Now try this

1 Name **three** things you need to be able to identify when analysing a text.

2 What is implied meaning?

Putting it into practice

You now know what to expect from the questions in the reading test. Prepare for your test by practising the following:

- reading different types of text and question
- underlining key information
- answering multiple choice questions
- answering short response questions.

Read the extracts from Text A and Text C and the test-style question below. Look at how a student has annotated the text and the question. The full version of Text A is on page 76 and Text C is on page 78.

✓ The student has underlined which texts they need to use.

✓ 'Different ideas' shows that the student needs to compare different points of view.

✓ Underlining 'example' reminds the student that they need to support their answer with evidence from the text.

✓ The student has highlighted some examples of activities we use technology for. In the text these are presented as not very useful.

✓ The final underlined sentence clearly links to the focus of the question. It suggests that technology is harmful and not useful.

✗ The student has underlined a statistic, but has missed the focus of the question. This sentence says nothing about the *usefulness* of using technology.

✗ The student hasn't underlined Text C. If a question instructs you to compare two or more texts, you will need to find information in both texts to support your answer.

> **10** Explain **two** ways Texts A and C have different ideas about the usefulness of technology.
>
> Give an example to support each answer.
>
> **(4 marks)**

Text A

It seems they do. According to research by the communications watchdog Comwatch, we spend more than 27 hours a week on the internet. Young people aged 14 to 18 spend a staggering 60 hours a week using technology such as phones and tablets. This means they spend half their lives staring at a screen, messaging their friends, watching videos and browsing social media.

This comes at a cost. Too much screen time can disrupt sleep, reduce the time we spend face-to-face with others, and make us less active. We are so attracted to our technology we hardly have time for anything else. It is like an addiction.

Text C

A new study found that using interactive technology can help develop hand–eye coordination. Computer games where children have to follow the action onscreen while using the mouse were found to be excellent preparation for writing and using tools such as scissors.

Computer games are also excellent for developing attention span. You might find your child's complete absorption in a game frustrating, but a study of 100 children found that 75% of regular gamers had a longer attention span than children who never played online.

Now try this

Re-read question 10 above, then read Text C on page 78. Identify and underline any parts of the text that would help you to answer the question. Remember to:

- skim read to find the most helpful part of the text
- avoid annotating too much text
- stick to the focus of the question.

Identifying the main idea

In your reading test you will need to identify the main ideas in a text.

Key parts of a text

This **headline** tells you the text is about young people, but does not say what is causing the misery.

The **first sentence** makes it clear that the main idea is young people who are homeless.

The **second paragraph** states that the number of homeless young people is rising. The word 'misery' in the title suggests that the detail in the text will be about how hard homelessness is for young people.

Text H

MISERY RISES FOR THE YOUNG

Government figures for the number of young people who are homeless are wildly inaccurate, according to research undertaken by a leading university.

The survey suggests that over 85,000 16- to 25-year-olds were homeless in 2014. This is over three times the number stated in the Government's official figures. The research calls the levels of homelessness 'a crisis', particularly as many young people are resorting to begging in order to feed themselves.

Reading further

Sometimes a title or heading suggests a clear main idea, but the first few sentences tell you that the text is not so simple.

This title does not make the main idea very clear – it could be talking about any generation.

The first two sentences make it clear that the main idea is young people's use of the internet. The writer appears to be critical of this.

The word 'actually' in the second paragraph suggests the text may be a bit more complicated.

Reading further, it seems the text is actually about how technology can benefit young people.

Text C

TECHNOLOGY – THE DIGITAL AWARENESS GENERATION

Are you dismayed by the amount of time young people spend on their phones and tablets? Do you criticise technology as a complete waste of time for children?

It may be time to stop moaning, as screen time may actually help to improve children's development.

A new study found that using interactive technology can help develop hand–eye coordination. Computer games where children have to follow the action onscreen while using the mouse were found to be excellent preparation for writing and using tools such as scissors.

Getting it right

In the test you must read the whole text carefully – not just the title and first few sentences. Important information can appear anywhere in the text.

Go to page 5 for more about skimming for detail.

Now try this

Look at Texts A, B and C (pages 76–78) on the topic of technology. For each one, write a sentence summing up the main idea.

Texts that instruct

For your reading test, you need to be able to recognise the purpose of a text. The purpose of some texts is to instruct. Texts that instruct tell the reader how to do something.

Type of text

Instruction texts can take many different forms, including recipes, manuals and directions.

- Recipes instruct the reader how to prepare a meal.
- Manuals instruct the reader how to make or use something.
- Directions instruct the reader how to get from A to B.

Language

You can recognise an instruction text by the following language clues:

- clear language that readers will be familiar with
- concise sentences that are quick to read and easy to follow
- command verbs telling you what to do, e.g. 'stop', 'turn off' and 'manage'.

Layout

1 Tables, bullet points and numbered lists are often used for instruction texts to show the information in the correct order.

2 Pictures and diagrams are sometimes used alongside written instructions to clarify what is meant.

Text E

Just a few simple steps can significantly reduce the fuel we waste in our homes, keeping bills low and reducing our impact on the planet.

What you can do:

1. <u>Stop</u> using standby mode. Teenagers are often the worst offenders here. Up to £80 a year can be saved just by getting them to switch their TVs and games consoles off at the socket.

2. <u>Turn off</u> lights. All it takes is the flick of a switch as you leave the room. Leaving a standard 60 watt bulb on all day will cost you about 10 pence; it doesn't sound like much but over a year it adds up.

3. <u>Manage</u> the temperature in each room. At any one time, half the rooms in your house could be sitting empty with the radiators on full blast. Install controllable valves on every radiator, and encourage teenagers to take responsibility for their room.

Purpose

This text wants readers to follow a 'few simple steps', which suggests it contains advice in the form of instructions. The main purpose of this text is to instruct, but it also informs the reader.

> Go to pages 31 and 32 for more about responding to a text.

Audience

Text E instructs the reader how to save money on their energy bill. This suggests that the audience is adults who own or rent accommodation.

The language used in Text E isn't particularly technical, which suggests that it is intended for a general audience rather than specialists.

jargon *noun*

vocabulary specific to a certain subject or profession that is difficult for others to understand

Similar words: technical language

Now try this

Look at the rest of Text E on page 80.

1 Find **two** more examples of command verbs.
2 Find **two** other reasons why the audience for the text is likely to be adults.

Texts that inform

Texts that inform use factual information to tell the reader something. Informative texts include leaflets, fact sheets and reports.

Language

Texts that inform usually use:

- formal language, such as 'vocabulary' and 'interactive', rather than slang
- factual information that can be proved to be true. Sometimes factual information can be presented in the form of statistics.

> Go to page 17 to read more about facts.

Layout

Informative texts, such as articles and reports, usually contain paragraphs to separate the main idea into detailed, relevant sections. The first paragraph usually contains the most important information. Here, the later paragraphs explain the ideas in more detail.

Paragraphs are sometimes separated by headings and sub-headings, which give the reader an idea of what the paragraph will be about.

Text C

TECHNOLOGY – THE DIGITAL AWARENESS GENERATION

Are you dismayed by the amount of time young people spend on their phones and tablets? Do you criticise technology as a complete waste of time for children?

It may be time to stop moaning, as screen time may actually help to improve children's development.

A recent study found that using interactive technology can help develop hand–eye coordination. Computer games where children have to follow the action onscreen while using the mouse were found to be excellent preparation for writing and using tools such as scissors.

Computer games are also excellent for developing attention span. You might find your child's complete absorption in a game frustrating, but a study of 100 children found that 75% of regular gamers had a longer attention span than children who never played online.

Active screen time also helps children develop language skills. By reading e-books and accessing stories online, they increase their vocabulary. Surprisingly, social networking sites can also be good for communication skills, giving young people the chance to express themselves creatively.

Purpose

The positive language and factual information suggest that the main purpose is to inform parents about the benefits of technology for their children.

Audience

The language here is formal and includes some complex vocabulary. The text refers to 'your child', so it is aimed at parents.

> ### Now try this

Read Text A on page 76. What is the **main** purpose of Text A? Support your answer with **two** examples for **each** of the following features:

- layout
- language.

Texts that persuade

When writing to persuade, writers use reasons and make clear points to try to get readers to believe or do something. Advertisements, articles, letters, leaflets and posters use persuasive writing.

Factual information

Persuasive writing often contains **facts** and **statistics**. These help to make the content believable and the writer seem like an expert. **Quotations** are used to add importance to writing. They help support the points being made and make them believable.

Language

Persuasive texts often use **descriptive language** to make the reader feel a particular way. In Text G, words such as 'damaging' and 'harm' suggest that giving money is not helpful, and 'pretty' makes us sympathise with the town of Knoswick.

Layout

In persuasive texts, each new point the writer makes should have its own paragraph.

Writers develop their ideas in an ordered and logical way to make it easy for the reader to follow. In Text G, the writer makes the point that giving money can encourage begging and affect towns, then suggests that not all money given to beggars is used for food and shelter.

Text G

Begging is illegal under the Vagrancy Act of 1824. However, it is not well <u>enforced</u> in many cities. Karim Akhtar, the Chief Constable of Broxtown Police Force, is determined to change this in his city. '<u>In response to concerns from the public, arrests for begging have increased by 50% over the past two years</u>', he stated.

Begging is not just a problem in big cities, either. Knoswick is a <u>pretty</u> town in the Estrick Hills that thrives on tourism. But begging is on the increase. '<u>It's our job to look our best. I worry what visitors think of the town, and how it will affect my business</u>', said hotel owner Nigel Shrike. Tourists who give money on the street encourage begging, and could ultimately be <u>damaging</u> local <u>livelihoods</u>.

You may think you're helping by giving to someone on the street, but you can't be sure that your money will be spent on essentials of life, such as food, clothing or shelter. Substance abuse is a common problem in the homeless community, so your kindness could do more <u>harm</u> than good. It's much more constructive to donate to a shelter, soup kitchen or homeless charity, where your money will fund proper care.

Purpose

This text wants to persuade readers that giving money to beggars is unhelpful, and that there are better ways to help the homeless. This suggests that the writer's main purpose is to argue that giving money to beggars does not actually help the homeless.

Audience

Text G uses some complex vocabulary, for instance 'enforced' and 'livelihoods'. This suggests that it is aimed at adults. More specifically, it is aimed at people who give, or are considering giving, money to beggars.

Now try this

Read Text C on page 78 and answer the questions below.
1 What does the layout suggest about the purpose?
2 What does the language suggest about the audience?
3 What does the writer want the reader to do?

Language techniques 1

In your test you will need to show that you understand how writers use different types of language to create different effects.

Read the extract from Text I on the right and look at the language the writer has used. Look out for:

Style

Think about whether the writer uses a serious, formal style, or a more personal, informal style. Here, the writer uses informal words to make the reader feel like the text is aimed at them. Informal phrases like 'rattle a tin' and 'pop your loose change' make the homeless shelter sound friendly and approachable.

Descriptive language

Descriptive language creates pictures in the reader's mind. Here, the writer has used the image of 'angels' to help persuade readers to become volunteers. The writer has also used descriptive language to make the volunteering roles sound worthwhile to the reader, such as 'sacrificing'.

Command verbs

These are verbs (doing words) that instruct an audience to act. Here, the writer tells readers to 'come and see us' to find out more.

Emotive language

Emotive words can appeal to the reader's emotions. Here, the words 'vulnerable' and 'make a difference' help to make readers feel sympathy for homeless people and encourage them to volunteer.

Text I

If you are interested in making a difference, Homeless Haven offers a range of volunteering opportunities to choose from.

Support Assistant Provide care and support for our guests by welcoming and advising them, and looking after their welfare throughout their stay.

Kitchen Assistant Work with our kitchen team to prepare tasty and healthy meals. Or if you prefer, work front-of-house and serve guests, help to clear tables and wash up after meals.

Outreach Homeless people are often isolated and unaware of the shelter and the help we provide. Get out on the streets with our team and reach out to vulnerable young people when they need us the most.

Fundraising Assistant

Collecting money is one of our most important volunteering roles, and it takes place outside all year round in all weathers. No real skill is required to rattle a tin outside your local supermarket, but the money given to us in this way is vital. If you can't spare the time to volunteer with us, then pop your loose change into one of our tins.

When are volunteers needed most?

Christmas Day is the most popular shift and opportunities are often filled weeks in advance. However, like many other charities, we need angels all through the year to fill our night-shift slots. Sacrificing a night's sleep, whether as a one-off or on a regular basis, would be a real help in our fight to keep our night shelters open.

How can you volunteer?

We are looking for volunteers who are able to commit at least a day per week. If this applies to you, come and see us to find out how you can become part of our team and make a difference to vulnerable people's lives. We are open 24/7.

Now try this

Read Text C on page 78. Explain **two** ways the writer's language convinces readers that using technology can have a positive effect on children.

Language techniques 2

Here are some more language techniques you may see in the test.

Repetition

Repeating the word 'We're' emphasises that the fuel crisis is something that affects everybody. Using the word 'We' also makes the audience feel that the writer is on their side.

Words or phrases are often repeated three times to add extra impact – this is sometimes called **the rule of three.**

Hyperbole

In this extract, the writer describes people 'sitting in a coat with the lights out'. This **hyperbole** (or exaggeration) emphasises the amount of effort people are making to save fuel.

Text F

We have all heard about the fuel crisis. <u>We're</u> urged to turn our heating down. We're nagged to turn our lights off. We're assured that this will save us money and help the environment. But does <u>sitting in a coat with the lights out</u> actually <u>make a real difference?</u>

Rhetorical question

A **rhetorical question** is asked not to get an answer, but to make the reader think. At the end of the extract the writer uses a rhetorical question to engage the reader and make them think carefully about fuel waste.

Counter-argument

Sometimes a writer will mention a different point of view to make their argument seem more balanced.

This writer acknowledges that hospitals should not be expected to turn down the heating. This **counter-argument** makes their argument more persuasive by making them seem sensible and caring.

Text F

<u>While nobody is suggesting that hospitals start turning down the heating and issuing more blankets,</u> it is shocking that public organisations such as schools, libraries and councils do not take fuel saving seriously.

Direct address

The writer can appeal directly to the audience by using 'you' – this is called **direct address.**

Here, the writer uses direct address to make the reader take action. This emphasises the writer's feelings about the way large organisations waste fuel.

Text F

So – next time <u>you're</u> in a public building, make a nuisance of yourself. Find somebody in charge and ask them why they're not following the example of the general public and doing something about the fuel crisis.

Now try this

Read Text C on page 78. Find **three** of the techniques described above and explain how they are used to convince readers of the benefits of technology.

Fact and opinion

Writers use facts, opinions and expert evidence to support their main ideas and argument. You need to be able to identify these correctly.

Fact

A **fact** is a statement that can be proved to be true. In this extract from Text G, the writer uses the fact that 'begging is illegal under the Vagrancy Act of 1824'. This gives the text authority and encourages the reader to trust the writer.

Factual information can be presented in the form of statistics, such as 'arrests for begging have increased by 50% over the past two years'.

> **statistic** *noun*
> a fact or piece of data collected from a study

Text G

BEGGING – TO GIVE OR NOT TO GIVE?

Begging is illegal under the Vagrancy Act of 1824. However, it is not well enforced in many cities. Karim Akhtar, the Chief Constable of Broxtown Police Force, is determined to change this in his city. 'In response to concerns from the public, arrests for begging have increased by 50% over the past two years,' he stated.

Begging is not just a problem in big cities, either. Knoswick is a pretty town in the Estrick Hills that thrives on tourism. But begging is on the increase. 'It's our job to look our best. I worry what visitors think of the town, and how it will affect my business,' said hotel owner Nigel Shrike. Tourists who give money on the street encourage begging, and could ultimately be damaging local livelihoods.

Opinion

An **opinion** is an idea or viewpoint that the writer believes is true. Here, the writer gives the opinion that 'this is not enough'. He then backs his opinion up with expert evidence.

> Go to page 21 to read about opinion and bias.

Text F

It seems it does. As a nation, domestic usage (and therefore wastage) of gas and electricity actually *dropped* in 2013 and is predicted to continue dropping at a rate of 0.5% every year for the next five years.

But this is not enough. According to Lily Xiao, Chairman of the World Energy Trust, we will exhaust our supply of fossil fuels before the end of this century unless we take drastic action to reduce our fuel waste. 'The irresponsible way we use fuel is not sustainable; if we do not act now it will be too late.'

Expert evidence

A writer might use **expert evidence** to make their argument more persuasive. This could be either a fact or an opinion from someone with expert knowledge on a topic.

Here, the writer quotes the Chairman of the World Energy Trust. This makes the writer's opinions seem sensible and realistic because they are supported by someone who knows a lot about the topic.

> Expert evidence can be direct speech or reported speech.
> - Direct speech gives someone's exact words in quotation marks.
> - Reported speech explains what someone said, but in the writer's own words.

Now try this

Read the rest of Text F on page 81. Find **two** more examples of facts and **one** more example of opinion.

Putting it into practice

In this section you have revised understanding and identifying:

- the main ideas in a text
- the main purpose of a text
- language techniques
- fact, opinion and expert evidence.

Look at the test-style questions below and read a student's answers.

Worked example

3 What is the **main** purpose of Text D?

It's about fuel waste.

(1 mark)

✗ The text is about fuel waste, but the student has not read the question carefully. The question asks the student to identify the **purpose** of the text.

Worked example

6 In Text E, 'Now we can relax and enjoy our cosily heated homes, can't we?' is an example of:

A reported speech ☐

B a statement ☐

C a rhetorical question ☒

D an exclamation ☒

(1 mark)

✗ The student has given two answers. The question is worth one mark, so only one answer is correct. No marks will be awarded, even if one of the answers given is correct.

Getting it right

If you change your mind about the answer to a multiple-choice question, don't worry. Put a line through the wrong cross, then mark your new answer with a cross.

Worked example

7 Identify **two** methods the writer of Text F uses to convince the reader that more should be done about the fuel crisis.

Give an example to support each answer.

1 The writer uses emotive language like 'drastic' to emphasise how serious the crisis really is.

2 'Surely this would be a perfect site for solar panels?'

(4 marks)

✓ In the first answer, the student has given an example, named the language technique and given a clear explanation that is linked to the question.

✗ In the second answer, the student has given an example, but has not named the language technique.

Now try this

Read Texts D, E and F on pages 79–81. Correct the mistakes made by the student in their answers above.

Implicit meaning 1

Writers can convey meaning in an explicit and implicit way. Something that is implicit is suggested, but not actually stated. You need to be able to identify and explain implicit meaning.

Interpreting implicit meaning

To identify implicit meaning, you will need to read the detail in the text very carefully. Read the extract on the right and think about the following key words and phrases:

- 'easier than ever' suggests that people find the internet very hard to resist
- 'waste hours' suggests that not everything online is worth watching
- 'slaves' suggests that people feel they are controlled by their technology
- 'fear of missing out' refers to people's worry that they will miss something important if they don't keep checking their messages.

So, the implied meaning of this text is that too much technology is not good for people.

Text B

With so much technology at our fingertips these days, it is <u>easier than ever</u> to <u>waste hours</u> watching funny videos of cats. Many people feel they have become <u>slaves</u> to their devices, checking their messages, reading the news and flicking through social media throughout the day for <u>fear of missing out.</u>

Always consider a word in context. This means thinking about what comes before and after – the **context** – to understand the implied meaning.

Creating an image

Writers often use implicit meaning to create an image to help readers enjoy and understand a text. Implicit meaning can also be used to influence readers' opinions in a subtle way, so that readers feel like they have made a decision about a topic themselves.
The key words and phrases in this extract include:

- 'hand in hand' – suggests that two things are very closely connected
- 'further stress' – suggests that the homeless face many challenges
- 'forcing them' – suggests they have no choice.

The implied meaning of these words and phrases suggests that life is hard and no help is available to young homeless people.

Text H

Living on the streets often goes <u>hand in hand</u> with other serious issues. Many young homeless people suffer from mental health issues, which they have to handle alone without proper treatment or support. And without a permanent address, they are unable to apply for work or benefits, adding <u>further stress</u> and <u>forcing them</u> to beg or steal to survive.

Go to pages 15 and 16 to revise different language techniques.

Now try this

Look at the words and phrases underlined in this sentence from Text H on page 83. Write **one** sentence about each word or phrase, explaining the implied meaning.

Text H

It also suggests that police should <u>prioritise</u> helping young people on the streets find a <u>safe place</u> to sleep, rather than <u>arresting them for begging</u>.

Implicit meaning 2

Questions about implied meaning can be tricky. Make sure you know how to approach them before the test.

Reading the question

Start by reading the question carefully, underlining key words to identify the focus of the question. This will give you an idea for what to look for in the text. For this question, you need to look for details about the way people use their heating.

> **9** Give **one** quotation from Text D and **one** quotation from Text E that convey the view that <u>fuel is wasted</u> by the way people <u>heat their houses.</u>
>
> **(2 marks)**

Reading the text

Skim read the first few sentences of each paragraph to find the relevant part of the text. Here, the second sentence mentions the 'fuel we pay for is wasted'.

Then, read the paragraph in detail for more information. This reveals our answer – 'many of us have our heating switched on day and night' **implies** that we waste fuel by leaving the heating on longer than necessary.

> ### Text D
>
> However, it is all too easy to blame rising fuel prices. Around a third of <u>the fuel we pay for is wasted</u>, mainly through inefficient or careless use of household appliances. We leave our TVs on standby, charge our phones and laptops overnight and light our houses as if it was Christmas all year round. We expect our homes to always be warm, so <u>many of us have our heating switched on day and night.</u>

Which is the answer?

There may be more than one suitable quotation to answer the question. Three of the numbered points in Text E contain information about how people heat their houses. Any of these could be used as a quotation to answer the question, as they all imply that people waste fuel when heating their houses.

> ### Text E
>
> **3** Manage the temperature in each room. At any one time, <u>half the rooms in your house could be sitting empty with the radiators on full blast</u>. Install controllable valves on every radiator, and encourage teenagers to take responsibility for their room.

Getting it right

Be careful when there is more than one suitable answer. Make sure you only include the number of quotations asked for in the question.

Go to page 24 to revise using quotations in an answer.

Now try this

Read the whole of Text D on page 79. Find **two** more quotations that could be used to answer question 9 above.

Point of view

Writers usually express a particular point of view about the topic they are writing about. In the test you may be asked to identify or compare points of view.

Identifying a writer's view

Question 1 on the right is asking what the writer believes. To work out the writer's point of view, think about:

- the facts – what do they suggest about the topic?
- the opinions – what do they suggest the writer feels about the topic?
- the language used – look for interesting words and phrases.

1 The writer of Text G believes that:
   A most beggars do not deserve our money ☐
   B the police are not doing enough to stop begging ☐
   C begging is decreasing in the UK ☐
   D most people who beg on the streets are homeless ☐

Facts

The following **facts** are based on findings recorded by the police, so they are reliable. They suggest that some beggars don't need the money.

Text G

Not all beggars are genuine. There is evidence to suggest that organised gangs may be running begging scams in some cities. Police have found 'professional' beggars working in Broxtown and Estrick, where their earnings are as high as £100 each per day.

Opinions

This is the writer's **opinion**. The phrase 'You may think' implies that the writer feels many people are wrong about how to help homeless people.

Text G

You may think you're helping by giving to someone on the street, but you can't be sure that your money will be spent on essentials of life, such as food, clothing or shelter.

Language

Language like 'pretty' and 'thrives' paints a picture of a beautiful place being spoilt by begging. This makes us less sympathetic to beggars in the town.

Text G

Knoswick is a pretty town in the Estrick Hills that thrives on tourism. But begging is on the increase.

Bias

This writer gives only one side of the argument. All the evidence about beggars is negative. This is called showing **bias**. Writers can also show their bias through exaggeration.

> Go back to pages 15 and 16 to revise language techniques.

> When looking at quotations, think about the implied meaning of individual words and phrases.

Now try this

1 Use the annotations above to work out the correct answer to question 1.
2 What does the following quotation from Text G suggest about the writer's view of begging?
   'Not all beggars are genuine.'

Putting it into practice

In this section you have revised:

- implicit meaning
- writers' point of view
- bias.

Read Text A on page 76 and look at a student's answers to the test-style questions below.

Worked example

1 The writer of Text A believes that:

A people cannot live without technology ☒

B too much technology can cause problems ☐

C young people need more sleep ☐

D technology is essential to modern life ☐

(1 mark)

✗ The text suggests that people may be addicted to technology, but not that they can't manage without it. The student needs to read the whole of the text, not just the beginning.

Worked example

2 In Text A, what do the following quotations suggest about <u>the writer's view of technology</u>?

'a bit of a dinosaur'

the writer thinks they are old-

fashioned so they don't see

technology as essential

'a crafty look at my texts'

feels guilty

(2 marks)

✓ The student has thought carefully about the implied meaning of the word 'dinosaur' in the quotation. They have given a full and detailed answer that is clearly linked to the focus of the question.

✗ The student's answer is too brief and general. 'confess' and 'crafty' do imply guilt, but the answer is not linked clearly enough to the writer's view of technology.

Getting it right

Always look at how many marks are available for the question. If there are two marks available for each answer, you need an example and an explanation.

Now try this

Read Text A on page 76 and answer questions 1 and 2 above.

As you read the text, remember to think carefully about:

- the facts – what do they suggest about the topic?
- the opinions – what do they suggest the writer feels about the topic?
- the language used – look for interesting words and phrases.

Using more than one text

For several of the questions in your test, you will need to use more than one of the texts. Follow these simple tips for using more than one text.

Comparing texts

 Read the questions carefully. Most questions will specify the texts you should use in your answer. For this question, you are asked to use Text A and Text C.

 Always look at the number of marks available. This question is worth five marks, so you will need a longer answer. Your answer will need to be balanced, so you should spend time selecting several points from each of the two texts.

 Make it clear which text you are writing about when you are giving examples.

Worked example

10   Using Text A and Text C, explain how these writers have different ideas about the benefits of using technology.

Support your answer with examples from each text.

<u>Text A</u> suggests that technology is damaging as it disrupts sleep and stops us taking exercise. However, Text C suggests that the internet can be very useful for young people's education…

(5 marks)

Choosing a suitable text

You could be asked to choose the most suitable text for a particular purpose.
For this type of question, you will need to read all the texts carefully and identify the pros and cons of using each text for the specified purpose.

For question 11, you need to choose **one** text that is:
• relevant to the topic
• suitable for the purpose and audience.
You need to provide evidence to support your answer, such as a quotation or a paraphrase.

> Go to page 30 to revise writing longer answers.

11   You are preparing <u>a presentation on how the internet can help you to learn a new skill</u>. Which text is the most useful to help with your presentation?

Give **one** reason for your choice and **one** example to support your answer.

(3 marks)

If you read all the questions before reading the texts, you will know what to look out for when reading for detail. This type of question will come towards the end of the test, so you should have read all three texts carefully by this point.

Now try this

Read the test-style question on the right, then answer the questions below.

1 Which text should you **not** use in your answer to this question?

2 Which **two** of the above tips would be most useful when answering this question?

8   Your friend does not believe that social networking has any benefits.

Using Text B and Text C, advise your friend on the ways social networking can benefit users.

(5 marks)

Selecting quotations

For many of the reading test questions you'll be asked to provide evidence from the texts.

Using quotations

 Underline any words that give the focus of the question.

 Read the text carefully, looking for key words and phrases that appear in the question.

 Underline the phrase that answers the question.

 Copy the quotation accurately and use inverted commas at the start and end.

You don't need to use the whole sentence in your quotation. Just make sure you use enough of the sentence to address the focus of the question.

Worked example

4 Give **one** quotation from Text E that <u>conveys the view that wasting fuel is damaging to the environment</u>.

'it also damages the environment'

(1 mark)

Text E

Wrong. Fuel waste is a massive problem in the UK. Not only does it cause debt misery for millions who struggle to pay their bills, but <u>it also damages the environment</u>. Just a few simple steps can significantly reduce the fuel we waste in our homes, keeping bills low and reducing our impact on the planet.

Using paraphrasing

If a question asks for evidence or an example, you can either use a direct quotation or put the text into your own words. This is called **paraphrasing**. Make sure you stick closely to the focus of the question when writing your answer.

Paraphrasing is effective when a question asks for examples, but if it asks for a quotation, you must copy directly from the text.

Text C

Computer games are also excellent for developing attention span. You might find your child's complete absorption in a game frustrating, but a study of 100 children found that 75% of regular gamers had a longer attention span than children who never played online.

Worked example

2 Explain **one** way the writer of Text C tries to convince the reader that using technology can be helpful for children.

The writer uses a counter-argument

by considering how parents might

be frustrated by how long their

children spend playing games.

(1 mark)

Now try this

Re-read question 2 above. Find another way that the writer of Text C tries to convince the reader that using technology can be educational for children. Either use a quotation or paraphrase the text in your answer.

Using texts 1

In your test you will need to show that you understand how to use the information in a text. This means reading carefully and selecting the most suitable information for a particular use or purpose.

Determining useful information

 A quick glance at this question suggests it is about young people who are homeless. Always read questions carefully – this is actually asking about **how to help** young people who are homeless.

 Skim reading suggests that Text H will be useful, because its title is 'Misery rises for the young' and it has a paragraph about 'dealing with the crisis'. Text I might also be useful as it is about volunteering and mentions clients who are under 25.

 Reading the texts carefully makes it clear that Text H is the most useful. Text I encourages people to volunteer at their local shelter, but Text H has the **most** information about how to help young people.

There are a total of three marks for this question. The answer is in three parts, so make sure you complete all of them to get full marks.

This question asks for an example, so include a quotation or a paraphrase in your answer.

Worked example

11 You are preparing a talk on how to help young people who are homeless.

Which text is the most useful when preparing your talk?

Give **one** reason for your choice and **one** example to support your answer.

Text Text H

Reason gives several ways to deal with problem of young homelessness.

Example making just one night a week of rough sleeping count as homelessness.

(3 marks)

Text H

MISERY RISES FOR THE YOUNG

The university survey puts forward several ideas for dealing with the crisis. These include changing the rules for local authority housing so that sleeping rough one night a week is enough to qualify as being homeless. It also suggests that police should prioritise helping young people on the streets find a safe place to sleep, rather than arresting them for begging.

Text I

Volunteering allows you to give something back to your community and help people who are less fortunate than you. Many of our clients are under 25, so it's a good opportunity to work with young people and help them secure a brighter future.

Getting it right

For questions about using information, you should follow the same steps as for other questions:

1 Read the question carefully and underline the focus.
2 Skim read the text to find the best places to look for information.
3 Go back and read the text carefully to make sure you find the correct answer.

Now try this

Read Texts G, H and I on pages 82–84. Follow the steps above to answer these questions:

1 Which **one** of the three texts would be most useful if you were preparing a presentation about how charities help homeless people?
2 Why would the text you have chosen be most useful?
3 Give an example to support your answer to question 2.

Using texts 2

One of the questions in your test will ask you to select information from each of the three texts.

Using all three texts

1 Read the question and underline the key words. The focus of this question is about fuel use. Reading carefully shows that you need to look for **advice** on how to reduce the amount of fuel we use.

2 Skim read each text to find the best places to look for the evidence. Look for key words from the question.

3 Read each of the sections you have found in more detail to find the most useful piece of evidence.

4 Double-check how many answers you need. This question asks for only one piece of evidence from each text, so don't be tempted to use more than one.

Worked example

12 You are giving a presentation about <u>how to reduce the fuel used in your area.</u>

Identify **one** piece of advice from **each** of the three texts about how fuel wastage could be reduced in your area.

Text D wear warm clothes at home so you can turn your heating down

Text E Turn off lights

Text F Put solar panels on schools

(3 marks)

> The question is asking for evidence from the text, which could be either a direct quotation or a paraphrase. This student has used a mixture of quotations and paraphrases.

Text D

Switching energy supplier is a good way to make savings on your fuel bills, and according to the Committee of Fuel Efficiency, consumers have already saved £2 million by switching suppliers. But chairman Stephen Chapman insists there is more we can do: 'We are still wasting fuel. <u>Putting on a jumper and turning the heating down could halve our winter bills.'</u>

Text E

1. <u>Stop using standby mode.</u> ...Up to £80 a year can be saved just by getting [teenagers] to switch their TVs and games consoles off at the socket.

2. <u>Turn off lights.</u> All it takes is the flick of a switch as you leave the room. Leaving a standard 60 watt bulb on all day will cost you about 10 pence; it doesn't sound like much but over a year it adds up.

Text F

My children's school, for example, is an impressive new building with carefully controlled heating and lighting that switches off automatically. But it still relies solely on gas and electricity for its energy. The school faces south and has a beautiful expanse of smooth sloping roof tiles. Surely this would be a <u>perfect site for solar panels</u>?

Now try this

Follow the steps above to find **one** piece of evidence from **each** of the three texts on pages 82–84 to persuade your friend to donate money to a homeless charity.

Putting it into practice

In this section you have revised:

• using quotations and examples

• using information from more than one text.

Look at the test-style questions below and read a student's answers.

Worked example

11   You are preparing <u>a presentation on internet safety.</u>

    Which text is the most useful when preparing your presentation?

    Give **one** reason for your choice and **one** example to support your answer.

    Text   Text B

    Reason   'Stay safe'

    Example   'anti-virus software'

                      (3 marks)

✔ The student has underlined the question focus.

✔ They have correctly identified Text B as the most useful – it has advice at the end about how to stay safe online.

✘ The student has confused 'reason' with 'example' and given a quotation. To get the mark here, the answer needs to say **why** the text is the most useful.

✘ They have used inverted commas but the quotation is too brief. The example needs to link clearly to the focus of the question and explain what anti-virus software has to do with internet safety.

Worked example

12   You want to know if <u>spending too long online is a risk to health.</u>

    Identify **one** piece of evidence from **each** of the three texts that suggests spending too long on the internet is a risk to health.

    Text A   'Too much screen time can disrupt sleep, reduce the time we spend face-to-face with others, and make us less active.'

    Text B   Looking at a computer too much is bad for your back.

    Text C   'even the most techno-savvy child needs fresh air every day!'

                      (3 marks)

✔ The student has underlined the question focus.

✘ This quotation is too long. It contains three pieces of evidence, not just the one asked for in the question.

✔ The student has correctly paraphrased a relevant part of Text B.

✘ This quotation doesn't fully link to the focus of the question.

Go to page 24 to revise selecting quotations.

Now try this

Read Texts A, B and C on pages 76–78. Look at both questions again carefully and correct the student's mistakes above.

Summarising 1

In the test you could be asked to summarise the ideas presented in the three texts.

summarise *verb*

give a brief statement of the main points of (something).

Example: 'these results are summarised in the following table'

Synonyms: sum up, condense, give an outline of, recap

Getting it right

Skim read the texts before you summarise them. When you first skim read a text it is a good idea to identify:

- the main ideas
- the writer's point of view about the topic.

Choosing the correct summary

You could be asked to choose the most accurate summary of texts from a list of options.

1 Read each of the options carefully.

2 Consider each one in turn: by the time you answer this type of question you should have read all three texts in detail and identified the main ideas and points of view.

3 Reject the options that are obviously wrong: statement C is easy to discount as only Text I is about volunteering.

4 If you are unsure about an option, go back and try to find evidence: only Text H is about statistics being unreliable; Text G is about young homeless people and Text I says **most** of their clients are under 25 – but neither text says that most homeless people are under 25.

13 Which statement below is an accurate summary of points made in the texts?

A Texts G and H both claim that statistics for homelessness are unreliable. ☐

B Texts G and I both suggest that supporting shelters is a good way to help the homeless. ☒

C Texts H and I both promote the idea of volunteering. ☐

D Texts G and I both state that most homeless people are under 25. ☐

Look at the verb given in each option. If you have identified a text as instructive, it is unlikely to 'argue'. This will help you to reject some statements.

Now try this

Read Texts A, B and C on pages 76–78. Follow the steps above to answer this test-style question:

13 Which statement below is an accurate summary of the points made in the texts?

A Texts A and C both state that using technology wastes time. ☐

B Texts A and B both argue that the internet can make life easier. ☐

C Texts B and C both claim that technology can save you money. ☐

D Texts B and C both promote different reasons for using technology. ☐

(1 mark)

Summarising 2

You could be asked to compare the similarities and differences of the three texts.

> **compare** *verb*
> note the similarity or difference between things
> *Example:* 'It is a good idea to compare menus before choosing a restaurant.'
> *Synonyms:* contrast, differentiate, distinguish

Comparing texts

1 First you need to identify the focus of the question by underlining key words or phrases. The focus of this question is the benefits of technology.

Read the question carefully. This question asks for **similarities**, not differences. It also asks for examples from **both** texts, so you would need to use quotations or paraphrases from Texts B and C.

> **10** Explain how Texts B and C present <u>similar</u> ideas <u>about the benefits of technology</u>.
>
> Give examples from both texts to support your answer.
>
> **(5 marks)**

2 Next, skim read the first text to find the best places to look for relevant information. This text has four points about how the internet can be a useful tool. This suggests that all four will be about the benefits of technology.

3 Then, skim read the second text to find ideas that are similar to those in the first text. The second text has a paragraph about 'skills'. This is similar to point 2 in the first text.

4 Finally, read both texts carefully and underline the similar ideas you have identified.

> **Text B**
>
> 1. **Use it to save money** Many retailers post offers and vouchers on social networking sites, so 'Like' your favourite shops to stay up to date with the best deals. You can also cut down on your phone bill by messaging your friends through social media instead of using texts and phone calls.
> 2. **<u>Learn a new skill or language</u>** There are loads of free apps out there that can help you learn <u>anything from Spanish, to DIY skills, to baking</u>.

> **Text C**
>
> Active screen time also <u>helps children develop language skills.</u> By reading e-books and accessing stories online, they increase their vocabulary. Surprisingly, social networking sites can also be <u>good for communication skills,</u> giving young people the chance to express themselves creatively.

Getting it right

If you are asked to summarise the writer's point of view, you should give a concise explanation and provide evidence from the text to support your answer.

Go to page 23 to read more about using more than one text.

Now try this

Follow the steps above to find **one** piece of relevant information for **each** text for the test-style question on the right.

> **10.** Read Texts A and B on pages 76 and 77. Explain how these texts have similar ideas about the effect of technology on people's health.
>
> **(4 marks)**

Writing a longer answer

For questions that are worth five marks, you will need to write longer answers and it is often helpful to write in full sentences.

Useful tips

To write a longer answer:

- identify how many points and examples you need to include
- stick to the point
- use signpost words and phrases to structure your answer
- use adverbials to signpost a comparison
- make it clear which text you are writing about.

Signposting your answer

Make your different points clear by using **signposting** words and phrases, such as:

One difference/similarity, Firstly, Secondly, Also

To introduce an example or quotation, use:

For instance, For example

Use adverbials to compare and summarise two texts:

Similarities – **similarly, likewise, both, in the same way**

Differences – **however, on the other hand, by contrast**

Example answer

Read Texts D and F on pages 79 and 80. Look at the test-style question and a student's answer on the right.

✓ This answer is clearly signposted. It is split into two short paragraphs and the word 'also' has been used. This makes it clear that more than one idea is being covered.

✓ Adverbials are used to clearly show the comparison being made.

✓ Examples have been given for each text.

It is important to stick to the point when writing a long answer. Use point–evidence–explain to help you to write a focused answer.

Getting it right

Practise writing longer answers under timed conditions before your test. Remember to be precise and concise so you don't spend too long on one question.

Worked example

10 Explain how Texts D and F present <u>different ideas about how to reduce fuel waste.</u>

Give examples from both texts to support your answer.

One difference is that Text D suggests that we can all reduce fuel waste by stopping our 'careless use of household appliances'. However, Text F suggests that government departments and public services need to reduce the waste as they do not 'take fuel saving seriously'.

Text D also suggests that fuel waste can be reduced by turning down our heating at home. On the other hand, Text F suggests that will not be enough. For instance, it states that we need to install solar panels and mini wind farms at our public buildings.

(5 marks)

This question asks for similarities. Signpost your answer using similarity adverbials – similarly, likewise, both, in the same way.

Now try this

Read Texts B and C on pages 77 and 78. Write an answer to the test-style question on the right. You could use the points identified on page 29.

10 Explain how Texts B and C present similar ideas about the benefits of technology.

Give examples from both texts to support your answer.

Responding to a text 1

For your test you will need to show that you understand how texts can be used to suit an audience's needs.

Understanding the audience

You will need to show that you can select and use relevant information from texts to suit the needs of a particular audience. Thinking about the purpose of the text will help – look out for information that is intended to advise the reader to do something.

> Go to page 45 to read more about audiences.

Getting it right

To answer questions about audience needs, you should follow the same steps as for other questions:

1 Read the questions carefully and underline key words.
2 Skim read the text to find the best places to look for information.
3 Go back and read the text carefully to find the details you need to write your answer.

Worked example

For questions like this, always identify both the audience and the focus in the question. The audience in this question is parents of teenage children, and the focus is heating bills.

4 Give **one** reason why Text E is the most useful for the parents of teenage children who want to reduce their heating bills.

Text E gives advice about encouraging teenagers to turn down the heating.

(1 mark)

A quick skim read of Text E reveals that the purpose of this text is to advise and there are two uses of the key word 'teenagers'.

Careful reading is always important. Only the second part of this extract is about heating. Two pieces of advice are given but the question asks for only one.

Text E

1. Stop using standby mode. Teenagers are often the worst offenders here. Up to £80 a year can be saved just by getting them to switch their TVs and games consoles off at the socket....

3. Manage the temperature in each room. At any one time, half the rooms in your house could be sitting empty with the radiators on full blast. Install controllable valves on every radiator, and encourage teenagers to take responsibility for their room.

Now try this

Read the rest of Text E on page 80. Follow the steps above to answer the test-style question on the right.

4 Give **one** reason why Text E is the most useful for a family who have to manage on a limited budget.

(1 mark)

31

Responding to a text 2

You will need to show that you are able to use more than one text to respond to an audience's needs.

Read the test-style question on the right and look at the student's annotations and answer.

The question does not tell you to use examples or quotations. However, it does say 'Using Text B and Text C', so it is important that you only use information from these texts. You should use quotations or paraphrase the text to support your answer.

> **8** Your friend does not think that there are any benefits to using social media.
>
> Using Text B and Text C, advise your friend on <u>the benefits of using social media.</u>
>
> **(5 marks)**

Text B

Skim reading suggests that these paragraphs will contain relevant information — the first one mentions saving money and the second talks about 'skills'.

1. **Use it to <u>save money</u>** Many retailers post offers and vouchers on social networking sites, so 'Like' your favourite shops to stay up to date with the best deals. You can also cut down on your phone bill by messaging your friends through social media instead of using texts and phone calls.

Text C

You should always read **the whole** of each paragraph carefully. Here the benefit of using social networking is actually stated in the final sentence.

Active screen time also helps children develop <u>language skills</u>. By reading e-books and accessing stories online, they increase their vocabulary. Surprisingly, social networking sites can also be good for communication skills, giving young people the chance to express themselves creatively.

✓ The student has used a clear structure for their answer.

✓ Starting with a short introductory statement makes it clear that you have understood the question.

✓ The student has identified both texts clearly.

> Go to page 30 to revise writing a longer answer.

Sample answer

Using social media has several benefits. For instance you can 'like' your favourite shops to hear about special offers (Text B). You can also use it to cut down on phone bills (Text B). Another benefit is that social media helps you improve your communication skills (Text C).

Now try this

Read the whole of Text C on page 78 and identify one more benefit of using social media. Use the example you identify to finish the answer to the test-style question above.

Putting it into practice

In this section you have revised:

- summarising information from more than one text
- using texts to respond to audience needs
- writing longer answers.

Read Texts G, H and I on pages 82–84. Look at the test-style questions below and read a student's answers.

Worked example

8 Your friend does not believe that the <u>homelessness situation is serious for young people.</u>

Using Text H and Text I, advise your friend on the seriousness of the homelessness situation for young people.

The homelessness situation for young people is very serious. For instance, 'over 85,000 16- to 25-year-olds were homeless in 2014'. Also, many young people have mental health problems and they need to beg as they get no benefits and getting a job is very difficult.

(5 marks)

> Writing to advise is similar to writing to persuade. You would need to inform your friend about the facts and explain them in a way that supports the statement in the question.

✓ This answer is well structured, with an introductory sentence and signpost words.

✓ This answer uses clear evidence from Text H in the form of quotations and paraphrasing.

✗ The student has only used Text H. It is a good idea to balance the answer by using two points from each of the texts. The question specifically instructs the student to use both Texts H and I.

Worked example

10 Use Text G and Text I to answer this question. Explain how these texts <u>have different ideas about people who beg.</u>

Give examples from both texts to support your answer.

Text G says people who beg spend the money on drugs. Some of the people who beg work for criminal gangs. Text I says people who beg are just like the people on your street or at your college. Text I says people who beg need help all year round.

(5 marks)

> Go to page 30 to revise how to write a longer answer.

✓ The student has used paraphrased examples from both texts and included two examples from each.

✗ The student has not structured the answer with signpost words or adverbials to show the comparison.

Now try this

Re-read both questions above.

1 Complete the answer to question 8 by adding points from Text I.
2 Rewrite the answer to question 10, using signpost words and adverbials to add structure.

Using a dictionary

You may already know how to use a dictionary, but here is a reminder.

Using a dictionary

Dictionaries are easy to use if you follow these rules.

- The words are in alphabetical order, so all the words beginning with **a** will be together.
- After finding the section for the first letter of the word, you need to look at the second letter – so **apple** will come before **arrow** as **p** is before **r** in the alphabet.
- The words are in bold to make them easy to find on the page.

Getting it right

Don't spend too long looking up words in the dictionary. Always try to work out the meaning of unfamiliar words by looking for clues in the surrounding text first. You could practise using a dictionary before your test by looking up any unfamiliar words you come across in this book.

Understanding a dictionary entry

This is the word you are looking up.

This is the definition, or meaning of the word – sometimes there is more than one meaning.

Dictionaries often show words that have a similar meaning to the word you have looked up. Looking at these can be the quickest way to work out a word's meaning.

dictionary *noun*

a book or electronic resource that lists words in alphabetical order and gives their meaning and examples of similar words

Similar words: vocabulary list, vocabulary, word list, wordfinder

Where to start looking

Look at the tricky vocabulary used in the text extract on the right. Follow the steps below to find the word **define** in the dictionary.

The word **define** begins with **d**, so you should look in the **d** section of the dictionary.

The second letter is **e**, which comes near the beginning of the alphabet, so the word will be found towards the start of the **d** section.

Some dictionaries give you an example of the word in a sentence.

Text H

Many young people are not legally defined as homeless.

define *verb*

state or describe exactly the nature, scope or meaning of

Example: 'My manager defined the responsibilities I would have in my new job.'

Similar words: explain, interpret, clarify

Now try this

Use a dictionary to find the meaning of the words **competitive** and **significantly** from Text E on page 80.

Avoiding common mistakes

During your test you will need to stay calm to avoid making simple mistakes. Look at the test-style questions and answers and tips below to help you to avoid common mistakes.

 Read the question

It is important to read the question carefully and stick to its focus. This student has focused on the **topic** of the text, not the **purpose**. The answer needs to identify what the text is for, not what it is about.

Worked example

4 Give **one** reason why Text E is the most useful for a person who has just moved house and has very little money to spend on improvements.

It's got tips about saving fuel.
....

(1 mark)

 Explain your answers

Look out for the word 'explain' in a question and check to see if you need to give an example.

This answer is just a paraphrase of the text. It does not explain what technique is used.

This answer correctly explains what technique is used, but does not give an example to support the explanation.

Worked example

7 Identify **two** methods the writer of Text F uses to convince the reader that more could be done to save fuel.
Give an example to support each answer.

1 drastic action is needed or we will have used up our fossil fuels

2 expert evidence is used

(4 marks)

 Read carefully

It is important to read each answer option carefully before making your final choice. Text D does mention changing fuel suppliers to reduce bills and Text E does have tips that will reduce fuel bills. However, the answer refers to **Texts D and F**, so it is incorrect.

> Go back to page 28 to revise this type of summarising question.

Worked example

13 Which of the statements below is an accurate summary of points made in the texts?

A Texts D and F both promote different ways of cutting our household bills. ☒

B Texts D and F both claim that domestic fuel wastage is rising dramatically. ☐

C Texts E and F both state that the environment is damaged by fuel waste. ☐

D Texts D and E both argue that fuel waste is not a serious problem. ☐

(1 mark)

Now try this

Read the questions on this page carefully. Underline key words in the questions, then read the texts in detail and correct the mistakes the student has made.

Checking your work

When you have finished answering the questions in your reading test, it is a good idea to go back over your answers to check for mistakes. This page will help you to spot some of the most common mistakes.

 Check your quotations

Check the question – if it asks for quotations, you must copy exactly from the text and use inverted commas.

✔ The student has given a relevant quotation from Text A.

✗ This student has given a paraphrase from Text C instead of a quotation.

Getting it right

It is a good idea to save 5 minutes at the end of the test to re-read the questions and check your answers.

Worked example

9 Give **one** quotation from Text A and **one** quotation from Text C which convey the view that young people spend too much time using technology.

Quotation from Text A

'young people are spending half their

lives staring at a screen'

Quotation from Text C

they seem to live online

(2 marks)

 Answer the question

This question asks for a reason and an example, not two examples.

Worked example

11 You are preparing a presentation about how large organisations do not take the fuel crisis seriously. Which text is the most useful when preparing your talk?

Give **one** reason for your choice and **one** example to support your answer.

Text F

Reason 'schools, libraries and councils do not take fuel saving seriously'

Example 'But it [the school] still relies solely on gas and electricity.'

(3 marks)

 Multiple-choice answers

This student has chosen two answers instead of one. Even though one is right, they would not get the mark for it.

Worked example

5 In Text E, the second paragraph beginning, 'Wrong. Fuel waste is a massive problem in the UK.' implies that people:

A realise how much fuel they waste. ☐

B are not wasting fuel in their homes. ☒

C know how much fuel they use. ☐

D are not aware that fuel waste is a problem. ☒

(1 mark)

Now try this

Read the questions on this page carefully. Underline key words in the questions. Then read the texts and correct the mistakes the student has made.

Writing test skills

For your Functional Skills writing test you will be given two writing tasks. These will test your writing skills, including spelling and punctuation.

Good writing skills

To do well in your writing test you need to:

- ✓ write clearly and concisely
- ✓ use details
- ✓ use suitable language for the audience and purpose
- ✓ present information in a logical order
- ✓ structure your writing
- ✓ use correct grammar, spelling and punctuation.

Writing skills in use

Look at the text extract on the right to see an example of good writing skills in practice.

Choosing the correct **style** of language is important. This text uses a formal style as the topic is serious and the writer doesn't know the audience.

Following **Point–Evidence–Explain** keeps your writing clear and concise. It will help the audience to understand your main ideas.

Using **sub-headings and paragraphs** gives structure to your writing and helps you express your ideas in a logical order. Remember, a new paragraph is needed for each new point or topic.

Including **complex sentences** and **adding detail** to your writing makes it more interesting for the audience and can help your writing achieve its purpose.

Using the pronoun 'you' makes the reader feel like you are addressing them directly. This is a particularly useful tool when writing persuasive texts.

HOMELESS HAVEN

Homeless Haven provides food, housing, support and friendship for the homeless across the UK. We transform the lives of vulnerable people, by providing somewhere safe and comfortable to stay and by helping them get back on their feet.

WHY SHOULD YOU VOLUNTEER?

People choose to volunteer for many different reasons. Volunteering gives you the chance to develop new knowledge and skills. It also offers the perfect opportunity to give something back to your community and help people who are less fortunate than you.

WHAT VOLUNTEERING OPPORTUNITIES ARE AVAILABLE?

If you are interested in making a difference, Homeless Haven offers a range of volunteering opportunities to choose from.

Support Assistant Provide care and support for our guests by welcoming and advising them, and looking after their welfare throughout their stay.

Kitchen Assistant Work with our kitchen team to prepare tasty and healthy meals, or if you prefer, work front-of-house and serve guests, help to clear tables and wash up after meals.

Getting it right

At the end of the test, check your writing to make sure you have used correct punctuation, spelling and grammar.

Now try this

1 Name **three** things you need to think about to do well in your writing test.
2 When should you use formal language?

Writing test questions

Read each task carefully to make sure you know exactly what you are being asked to do.

Writing test questions

You will need to answer two questions in your writing test. Each question will include an information section and a task:

- The **Information** section will give you a bit of background about a particular topic.
- The **Writing task** will explain the audience, purpose and format of your answer.

Audience, purpose and format

Before you start writing, you need to know what audience, purpose and format you are working with. Look at the test-style task on the right and the notes below.

 Audience

The audience may be just one person or many different people. Identifying the audience will help you to decide whether to use a formal or an informal writing style.

 Purpose

The purpose may be given in the first sentence of the task, or you may have to work it out from the bullet points. In ths task, you will need to use writing techniques to describe and explain.

 Format

The format will always be given. You could be asked to write a letter, an article, a report, an email or a review. You will need to use the correct style and layout for the format.

Go to pages 43 and 44 for more about writing for a purpose.

TASK B

Information

Lately there has been a problem with people leaving litter in your local park. You decide to write an article about it for your school/college/community newsletter.

You make the following notes:

- usually litter is soft-drink cans and fast-food containers
- spoils lovely community area for everybody
- litter is a health risk
- costs local councils millions of pounds a year to clear up
- litter is a hazard on pavements
- litter is a serious danger to wildlife in parks and nature spots.

Writing task

Write an article for your school/college/community newsletter. In your article you may:

- describe the issue of litter in your local park
- explain why it is a problem
- state what you think should be done about it.

You may include any other ideas.

Remember to write in sentences and use Standard English.

(15 marks)

Now try this

Look at Task B on page 86. Identify and underline the audience, purpose and format.

Letters, emails and reports

To make sure your writing is suitable, you will need to use the correct format for each task.

Letters

Your address and the date go on the right at the top of the letter.

The name and address of the person you are writing to go lower down on the left.

You can use a heading to draw the reader's attention to your topic. The language needs to be clear and formal.

Your letter should start with a short introductory paragraph giving the reason why you are writing.

At the end of a letter you need to use 'Yours sincerely' followed by a comma. Your name goes underneath.

> 4 Forest Road
> Burstown
> BR2 4HH
>
> Lev Petrov
> Venture Volunteering
> 4 Forest Lane
> Burstone
> BG1 4HH
>
> 27th April 2016
>
> Dear Mr Petrov
>
> **Volunteering Opportunities**
>
> I am writing to ask you about…
>
> I look forward to hearing from you.
>
> Yours sincerely,
> Ola Galetti

Emails

If you are asked to write an email, make sure you:

- add a subject heading summarising what the email is about
- use 'Dear' at the start of a formal email and 'Hi' at the start of an informal email
- end in a more informal way with 'Regards', or 'Thanks' if you are asking for something.

Reports

The title is formal and factual.

The report starts with an introduction giving the main facts about the topic.

Then it explains what the current situation is.

> **School Fundraising Events**
> Most schools in the country hold fundraising events…
> Our school currently has a non-uniform day for a local children's charity but does nothing at any other time of the year…

Next is a recommendation about what should change.

To conclude it summarises the advantages of the recommendation.

> I am proposing that we hold an annual school marathon event…

> So, a school marathon event would raise thousands for a worthwhile local charity….

Reports are information texts and should be formal and factual, but you will probably need to give your opinions too.

Now try this

Which format would be the most suitable for the following tasks?
1 Contacting the head teacher of a college to ask for a non-uniform day.
2 A proposal to install fitness equipment at your local park.
3 An answer to a request from a friend about good restaurants in your area.

Articles and reviews

Articles and reviews are formal pieces of writing intended to inform the reader. In the test, you may be asked to write an article or a review for a newspaper or newsletter.

Articles

The headline should give enough information to engage the reader. It might use a rhetorical question or a challenging statement to grab the attention of the audience.

The introduction summarises the key ideas in the article.

Sub-headings give more information to draw the reader in and help to organise the writing.

Expert evidence like statistics makes the article seem factual and reliable.

Teenagers: humans or hoodlums?

Not all teenagers hang around on street corners, swigging alcohol and being rude to passers-by. A new survey suggests that many young people today are valuable members of the community.

<u>Charity work</u>

52% of the teenagers surveyed had taken part in some form of charity fundraising over the last year.

> Go to pages 43 and 44 for more on using expert evidence and other writing techniques.

Barbara's Bistro: a long wait but a brilliant burger!

Barbara Neville only opened her bistro six months ago, but it has already become the first choice for many visitors to Rudwell town centre.

The menu is extensive and caters for all tastes. The speciality of the house is 'Barbara's Burger', which comes with a mind-blowing choice of over 40 different sauces! I chose the...

By the time my burger arrived I was ready to eat the table napkins!

Reviews

Reviews contain your opinions, so the style can be less formal than that used in an article.

The title usually gives some idea of your opinion.

An engaging opening gives the reader an idea about whether the review will be positive or negative, and makes them want to read on.

Further paragraphs add detail about the place or event being reviewed and begin to explain your opinion.

> This structure is suitable for any type of review. This is for a restaurant, but in the test you may be asked to review an event, a film or a place.

Now try this

Go back over the formats on this page and on page 39. Make yourself a revision table like this so that you know the correct structure for each format.

Format	Structure
Letters	
Articles	
Emails	
Reviews	
Reports	

Speeches

You may be asked to write a speech to be delivered to your school, college, workplace or in front of your local community. When writing a speech it is important to think about how it would sound spoken out loud.

Writing a speech

- Your opening sentence needs to grab your audience's attention. This example uses a rhetorical question, but you could also start with a bold statement, such as 'People should be publicly shamed for littering.'

- Use words like 'you' and 'we' to make your audience feel involved. This is called direct address.

- Speeches should be laid out in paragraphs, with a new paragraph for each new idea.

- Think about how your speech will sound. Short sentences are easier to say, and will keep your audience's attention. You could also use alliteration or repetition to make key sentences stand out.

- Back up your points with facts and statistics to make them sound more trustworthy.

- Use engaging language, but also make sure your point of view is very clear.

- The ending of a speech should be persuasive and memorable. Here, a short sentence has been used to address the audience and call them to action. Speeches can also end with warnings or a thought-provoking question.

Are you sick of looking out from your bench in the park at a carpet of litter? Unfortunately, litter now seems to be part of life in Britain. It is so common a sight that you might not even notice it very much.

However, it doesn't only spoil our views. Litter costs our councils millions of pounds a year to clear up. Over 60% of the litter on our streets and in our parks is soft-drink cans and discarded food containers. I think it is time we forced retailers and fast-food companies to take action.

So don't just sit there. Get out and do something about the menace of litter on our streets.

Go to pages 56 and 57 for more about language techniques.

Getting it right

Remember that a speech is meant to be spoken out loud. It can be hard to follow complicated arguments if they are spoken rather than written, so structure your speech very clearly. Look at the question carefully to find out who the audience is and decide how formal the language should be.

Now try this

The head of your college has proposed that all students should wear uniforms from now on, and has asked for students' opinions. Write a speech to advise him why you would or wouldn't want to wear a uniform.

Putting it into practice

You now know what to expect from your writing tasks, what skills they will test and what formats you will have to use. Read the test-style question below and look at how a student has prepared. You do not have to answer the question.

Task A

Information

You read the following advert on a social networking site.

Community Funding needs your help!

We need help in the following areas:

- running stalls at weekly bring-and-buy sales
- delivering leaflets locally to advertise our fundraising events
- competing at our sponsored swimming and running events
- serving refreshments at our events
- acting as fundraising treasurer.

All money raised goes to local causes. So far, we have bought the kit for the local boys' football team and paid for the community centre to be re-decorated.

Any skills or previous experience would be very welcome but are not essential. If you have enthusiasm and spare time we will find something for you to do!

If you are interested, write an email to sylvie@communityfunds.net

👍 Like   💬 Comment   ⬍ Share

Sample answer

Subject: Volunteering for bring and buy sales

Dear Sylvie,

I would like to volunteer to help with the Community Funding bring-and-buy-sales.

I have lots of experience working on my uncle's market stall at the weekends, so am confident chatting with customers and handling money.

I am studying fashion at college, so would be particularly interested in helping on the clothes stall.

My friends and I spend a lot of time in the community centre, and my little sister plays for the local football team. I'd really like the chance to give something back and support the charity.

Regards,

Richard Cho

✓ The student has thought about format. He has added a subject line, started with 'Dear' and signed off with 'Regards'.

✓ The language is more relaxed than a letter, but still fairly formal because he is writing to a stranger.

✓ He has said that he is interested in helping on the clothes stall, and has explained why.

✓ He has described his experience and the qualities that make him suitable for the role.

Now try this

Try writing your own email to Sylvie, volunteering and explaining your idea for a coffee stall at the bring-and-buy sale.

Inform, explain, describe, review

For both writing tasks you will need to demonstrate that you can use a range of writing styles and features for different purposes, such as informing, explaining, describing and reviewing.

Writing to inform

When writing to inform, you should use clear, simple language and sentence structures. You should add detail, but remember to be concise.

Facts and **statistics** make your informative writing seem trustworthy and reliable. Use facts and statistics as evidence for your points. You can make up facts and statistics in your test, but they need to be believable!

It is also important to think about layout. **Headings** and **sub-headings** will help you to organise informative writing, and present information to the reader in a logical way. Use sub-headings to make the topic of your paragraph clear.

Bullet points are a good way to break up a list of facts or points in an argument.

Writing to explain

When writing to explain, use clear and simple language to help the reader understand your topic. Assume that your audience does not know much about the topic and explain any technical terms.

Use **command verbs** such as **stop, go** and **ask** to get information across effectively and encourage the reader to take action.

If you are writing instructions you could use bullet points or a **numbered list** to break up the stages and make them easier to follow. Alternatively, **adverbs** such as **first**, **also**, **next** and **finally** will help guide the reader through the text. These can also be useful in informative writing.

Writing to describe

When you are describing, you want to create a picture in the reader's mind. Use effective language to help you do this:

* Adjectives and adverbs add detail

  he walked away casually

* Similes compare things and add imagery

  the water was like a mirror

* Metaphors create a dramatic image

  that girl is a star

You can help the reader feel like they are really there by focusing on senses and emotions. Think about the following ideas:

* How does this place make you feel and why?
* What does it smell like?
* Can you hear anything?
* Is it hot or cold?

Writing to review

In a review, you are giving your opinion, so you may use a less formal style. However, it is important to give a **balanced** perspective and back up your points with evidence.

Comparison can be a useful feature when writing a review. Use **connectives** such as **whereas**, **though**, **equally** and **however**.

You usually wouldn't use bullet points or sub-headings in a review, but you still need a title. Choose something eye-catching and engaging that will make people want to read on.

For all of these different purposes, the style you use will depend on your audience.

Now try this

Look at the test-style task on the right, then complete the tasks below:

1 What can a heading or title help you to identify?
2 Write down two facts and two statistics you could use in the article.
3 Write one sentence about the style and language you could use in this article.

Write an article for your school/college/community newsletter.

In your article you may:

* describe the issue of litter in your local park
* explain why it is a problem
* state what you think should be done about it

You may include any other ideas.

43

Argue and persuade

In persuasive writing you need to convince your audience to share your opinion. A successful persuasive text uses powerful language features and carefully thought out arguments.

Key points

A persuasive text should be based on a few key points. A good way to structure your argument is to choose one point about what is wrong with the way things are, then follow it up with ideas of how to make things better.

Try to use one paragraph for each of your points. If you have a list of shorter points, you could highlight them with bullet points instead.

Use adverbs such as **firstly**, **secondly**, **also** and **for instance** to link your ideas and create a clear argument.

Counter-arguments

In persuasive writing you need to express your point strongly, but it is also important to show that you have thought about both sides of the argument.

A **counter-argument** is where you mention how the reader might disagree with you, and then defend your point of view against it.

You may think that cyclists are a danger to pedestrians and drivers, but police statistics show that last year just two accidents in Estrick were caused by riders.

Language techniques

Use language techniques to influence your audience:

Rhetorical questions

Surely there has to be a better way?

Direct address

All you have to do is get out there and give it a go!

Lists

Parked cars, huge lorries, impatient drivers – the dangers are endless!

Alliteration

Cycling is fun, free and fantastic for your fitness!

Emotive language

Just last week my friend had a terrifying experience on the roads.

Evidence

Always support each of your key points with evidence, such as:

Facts and statistics

Over 60% of car journeys are under five miles

Expert opinions

Bonnie Cross, chairman of Cycling North West, says that better facilities are the answer: 'Cycling to work is on the increase, but many people are put off by the lack of secure cycle parking and showers at work.'

Examples from your own experience

I was cycling to my friend's house the other day, and the cycle lane just disappeared from the road!

Now try this

Look at the test-style task and then complete these tasks.

1 Note down **three** key points you could use in your answer.

2 Think about how your audience could disagree and make a counter-argument.

Your council is planning to close a local park because of complaints about young people using it at night. Write a letter to Ms Sophie Green, Broxtown Council, 3 Oak Lane, Broxtown, BR2 5NG.

In your letter you should:

• state whether you agree or disagree with the Council's proposals

• give detailed reasons to support your views

• state clearly what action you want the Council to take.

Audience

In the test you need to think about the audience you are writing for. It is important to make sure that your writing is suitable for your audience and gives the information they need to know.

Specific or general?

You need to know how to write for both a specific and a general audience.

- Reports, articles and reviews have a **general** audience – they could be read by many different people. When you are writing for a general audience like for Task F, you still need to think about their needs, and likes and dislikes.

- Letters and emails usually have a **specific** audience. For Task G on the right, you need to include an appropriate greeting and sign-off, and use direct address.

Do you know the audience?

How well you know your audience and what your relationship is to them will affect how you write to/for them.

- For an individual you know well, such as a friend (Task G on the right), you can use an informal style.

- For someone you don't know well you should always use a formal style.

- For a general audience think about the context, and choose a formal style if you are unsure.

Choosing an audience

The task on the right instructs you to choose an audience from three different options. Choosing the audience you can relate to most will make it easier to write to/for them. For example, if you are a student, you will find it easier to relate to other students.

> **Knowing** an audience and **knowing about** an audience are very different. You can write about things you know the audience will like but you still need to be fairly formal.

Task F

Write an article for the *Broxtown Local News*, describing your life-changing moment in detail.

In your article you should:

- say when your life-changing moment happened
- describe the occasion or experience that was life-changing
- explain what made it life-changing for you.

Remember to write in sentences and and use Standard English.

Task G

Write an email to your friend, persuading them to take part in the Technology Detox challenge.

In your email you should:

- give detailed reasons why your friend should take part in the detox
- explain exactly what the detox involves
- describe the benefits of taking part.

Remember to write in sentences and and use Standard English.

(15 marks)

Task H

Write a report for your school/college/workplace on how to spend the grant money. In your report you should:

- suggest which of the canteen areas needs improvement and why
- explain exactly what improvements should be made
- explain how the improvements will benefit everyone.

Remember to write in sentences and use Standard English.

(15 marks)

Now try this

Read Tasks F, G and H above and think about the audience. Write **three** important points to consider about each of the audiences.

Formal writing

You should read the writing task information carefully to work out how formal your writing should be. Letters, articles and reports will need to use a formal writing style. Emails and reviews can be more informal.

Formal writing

You should use a formal style if:

- you are applying for a job
- you do not know your audience well
- your purpose is official, for example making a complaint
- you are writing to somebody official, for example a recruitment agent
- you are writing an article or a letter to someone you don't know.

Using Standard English

When writing a formal text, you should use Standard English, which means using:

- complete words ('I am')
- complete sentences
- correct punctuation and grammar.

You should avoid:

- text language, e.g. 'LOL'
- slang, e.g. 'I was gutted'
- contractions, e.g. 'I'm'

Writing a formal letter

Read the test-style task extract on the right, based on Task E (page 89) and look at a student's answer.

> Go to pages 59 and 60 to revise sentences.

Write a letter to Ms Talia Albert, Head of Planning, Broxtown Council, 3 Oak Lane, Broxtown, BR2 5NG.

In your letter you should:

- state whether you agree or disagree with the Council's proposals
- give detailed reasons to support your views
- state clearly what action you want the Council to take.

Remember to write in sentences and use Standard English

If you do not know if a woman is **Miss** or **Mrs**, you should use **Ms**. Never use a first name in a formal letter.

Notice how 'I am' is written in full.

Complete sentences are used.

If you are handwriting the letter, you should start a new paragraph on a new line and write the first word further to the right.

If you are typing a letter, leave a blank space between the paragraphs.

Sample answer

Dear Ms Albert,

I am writing to give you my views about your proposal to close Broxtown Leisure Centre.

I strongly disagree with your proposal. The Leisure Centre is a vital community facility that is used regularly by many local residents.

Now try this

Read the information for the task above on page 89. Write **two more** sentences of the letter, using formal language.

Informal writing

In your writing test, you need to work out whether your answer should be formal or informal. This page explains when and how you should use informal writing.

When to use informal writing

You can use an informal writing style if:

- you know your audience personally
- your purpose is to be friendly, for instance if you are asking for help or sponsorship
- you are using an informal format, like an email or an internet discussion
- you are writing a review and want to address your audience directly.

Writing informal answers

When using informal writing, you should use:

- informal contractions, e.g. 'don't' or 'can't'
- informal phrases
- correct grammar and punctuation
- correct spelling
- complete sentences
- specific text features.

Writing informal emails

When the email audience is a friend, the greeting can be informal, for example 'Hi'. For people you do not know, it is better to use 'Dear'.

Look at the test-style task on the right, based on Task G on page 91.

Writing task

Write an email to your friend, persuading them to take part in the Technology Detox challenge.

In your email you should:

- give detailed reasons why your friend should take part in the detox
- explain exactly what the detox involves
- describe the benefits of taking part.

Remember to write in sentences and use Standard English.

Sample answer

Hi Hannah,

You should take part in the Technology Detox challenge with me. We could both do with a break from spending so much time online on our laptops.

For the challenge, we would need to give up technology for one hour every day in March. We could start going to a dance class, if you'd like to?

We'd be giving our eyesight a break from staring at the screen for so long and improve our posture. Let me know if you fancy the challenge!

Regards,

Liam

Notice that this email is informal, but the student still uses complete sentences. The student has used informal language here. If you are using slang words or phrases, make sure you know the reader will understand them.

Always remember to sign off a letter or email. When the email audience is a friend, you can sign off with 'Thanks,' or 'Regards,'.

Exclamation marks are a good way to show excitement in an informal format like an email. Don't use too many as they will lose their impact.

Now try this

Read the information for the task above on page 91. Then write **two more** sentences of the email, using an informal writing style.

Putting it into practice

In your writing test, you will need to show that you understand:

- the audience
- the type of text
- the purpose
- formal and informal texts.

Read the test-style task below, based on Task B on page 86, and look at how a student has answered.

Getting it right

If a question gives you a choice of audience, make it clear which audience you have chosen. You can do this by using information that suits your chosen audience.

Task B

Write an article for your school/college/community newsletter.

In your article you may:

- describe the issue of litter in your local park
- explain why it is a problem
- state what you think should be done about it.

You may include any other ideas.

The information in an article should sound reliable and trustworthy. Formal writing is the best way to do this.

Sample answer

Litter

Broxtown has a beautiful park with a bowls green, tennis courts and a well-equipped play area for local kids. The park is a wonderful community area for the whole family. Parents can spend whole days in the park as there is so much to keep their kids busy.

It's great to have a place like this to hang out with your friends at night. It's safe and well lit so your Mum doesn't kick off when you spend summer nights there with your mates. Chilling out at the park is what the school holidays are all about!

That's why it's a shame that all this is being ruined by the litter that appears in the park every morning.

✗ A title has been used, but it is not interesting enough for an article. No sub-headings have been used.

✗ The audience is not clear. The article starts with a list of three attractions at the park that suit all ages. The first paragraph seems to be addressed to parents, making it suitable for a community newsletter. However, the second paragraph is addressed to teenagers, suggesting that the article is for a school-aged audience.

✗ The informal phrase 'kick off' would be acceptable in an email to a friend, but it is not suitable for an article.

✗ The style is incorrect. Words like 'kids' and 'chilling' are too informal for an article. The student has also used 'it's', 'doesn't' and 'that's', which are not formal enough for a formal article.

Now try this

Read the information for the above task on page 86. Rewrite the student's answer:

1 Choose a suitable title and sub-headings for the article.
2 Use the correct formal style.
3 Make the audience clear.

Planning

Before you start writing, it is a good idea to make a plan. This will help you to:

- make sure your writing suits your audience, purpose and format
- develop your ideas with suitable detail.

Informed planning

Before you start planning, read the task and the information section carefully. Some tasks have bullet points that you can use as a starting point for your plan.

In your plan you should include brief notes on the audience and purpose, and any key information you want to include. Don't spend too much time writing your plan. You can put all the detail you want in your answer.

Writing a good plan

To write an effective plan:

1 read the task and the task information carefully

2 underline audience, purpose and format

3 underline information in the task that will help you with your answer

4 use the bullet points to structure your plan

5 use the information you have underlined in the task to add ideas to your plan.

Example plan

There are different ways you can plan your writing. Choose one that suits you. Look at how a student has used the information in Task G on page 91 to plan their answer, below.

Go back to page 39 to revise writing an email.

Task G

Write an email to your friend, persuading them to take part in the Technology Detox challenge.

In your email you should:

- give detailed reasons why your friend should take part in the detox
- explain exactly what the detox involves
- describe the benefits of taking part.

Remember to write in sentences and and use Standard English.

(15 marks)

Sample answer

Email. Can be informal as it is to friends. Add subject heading and use 'Hi' as greeting.

- all spending too long online, couch potatoes
- health problems – use research, back problems, eye damage, no exercise
- detox = just one hour a day for one month, all exercise together
- better health, more time for other things

Getting it right

On the online test you can use the notepad to write planning notes. None of the notes you make here will be marked.

You can tick off each item in your plan as you write to check that you have covered everything.

Now try this

Look at Task J on page 94. Using the tips above, use the bullet points in the task to start a plan that will help you to answer the question.

Using detail

All the writing tasks start with an information section. You should use this information to add detail to your writing. This will help you to give your audience all the information they need.

Where to use detail

Read the information section to help you think of ideas for your writing. If the task has bullet points, read them and then skim the information section for relevant details.

You should also use your imagination to think of details you can add to your writing to make it interesting to read.

Adding detail to your points

Read Task G on page 91 and look at a student's detailed plan on the right. This plan uses a list, but you can use a spider diagram if you prefer. Number your points so that you have a clear structure.

This plan has:

1 **an introduction** that makes the topic clear and uses information from the question

2 **a clear structure** using the bullet points from the question

3 **features suitable for format** – sub-headings make the information in a report clear and easy to follow

4 **features suitable for purpose** – this student is planning to use facts and statistics to make the information seem trustworthy and reliable

5 **detail** – extra ideas have been added to each point: these are not in the information section of the task, but they are suitable for the audience that has been chosen.

Sample answer

Plan
• Report for workplace
• Must be formal and serious
1 <u>Introduction</u>: canteen facilities, report into use of £10,000 grant
2 <u>Existing facilities</u>: no hot food, little choice, problem for those working long hours. Use facts from survey of staff.
3 <u>Improvements suggested</u>: hot food area – serving area, pasta and jacket potato bars. Use statistics to give costs of this improvement, save money.
4 <u>Benefits</u> all employees' work shifts, difficult to get hot meals on very early and very late shifts (use statistics from survey to prove this point). Work better if properly fed = benefit for company and staff. Money left over could be spent on decorating or pictures to make canteen more cheerful place = make staff even happier.

Now try this

Look at Task F on page 90. Follow the steps above to plan an answer. Remember to plan for features suitable for the purpose of your writing.

Paragraphs

For both your writing tasks you will need to show that you can structure your work.

One way to structure your writing is to use paragraphs. A paragraph is a group of sentences about one topic or idea. By grouping your ideas into paragraphs, you can develop each point with detail. Letters and articles always need paragraphs.

Planning the structure of a text

Look at a student's plan (below) and answer (on the right) for Task A on page 85.

1 Short intro – why I am emailing

2 Run vintage clothing stall – vintage clothes sell well as they are fashionable. People can bring stuff. Donate my own items.

3 Running – organise sponsored run. Take part in 5k park run. Get running club involved. Running popular = lots of donations.

4 Treasurer – qualified accountant. Work for local companies/Scouts.

This plan has been used to write four separate paragraphs. Each paragraph is about a different idea or topic.

Make your paragraphs clear: always start a new line for each paragraph. You could leave a whole line clear between each of your paragraphs.

Using a topic sentence

Start each paragraph with a topic sentence – a sentence that clearly introduces the reader to the content of the paragraph. Use the remaining paragraphs to develop and add detail to the idea in the topic sentence.

I am emailing you in response to your advertisement on Broxtownchat.co.uk, as I am interested in helping with your community fundraising.

I notice you are asking for volunteers to run stalls at your weekly bring and buy sales. I think a vintage clothing stall would be a good idea because retro and vintage clothes are very fashionable at the moment. We could ask people to bring their own old clothes for us to sell on the stall, and I would also be happy to donate some of my best vintage items.

A sponsored run is also something I am happy to organise. I run regularly and take part in the local 5k park run every Saturday morning. When I tell my friends from the park run about community fundraising, I'm sure they will want to be involved. Running is very popular now, so a sponsored run should bring in a lot of donations.

I see from the details on your advertisement that you need a fundraising treasurer. Last year, after two years at Broxtown College, I qualified as an accountant and am now working for a local company. I look after the accounts for several local companies and act as treasurer for the Broxtown Scouts. I'd be more than happy to do the same for your community fundraising group.

Now try this

Look at a student's ideas for Task C (page 87) on the right.

1 Structure them into a paragraph plan like the one above.

2 Write one of the paragraphs and make sure:
   • you use a clear topic sentence
   • you add detail to develop the idea in the topic sentence.

Playground damage, swings broken, no sign about dangers, nature trail interesting and guide informative, children disappointed, litter on paths, large menu, long wait for hot food, muddy walkways, no ice cream

Point-Evidence-Explain

You can structure your paragraphs effectively by using Point–Evidence–Explain (P.E.E.). P.E.E. helps you to add detail to your writing and keep it organised.

What is Point-Evidence-Explain?

For every paragraph you should:

- make your point in the first sentence.
- provide evidence to support your point – this can be more than one sentence if you have a lot of details to add
- explain how the evidence backs up your point.

Evidence

Your evidence should include facts and details.

You could use:

- details from the task information
- facts and statistics from other sources
- facts about your own personal experience.

Getting it right

P.E.E. will help you with both your writing tasks. Remember to read the task information carefully to find ideas that you can use as evidence.

Using P.E.E. to add detail

Look at the paragraph from a student's answer to Task J (page 94) on the right.

1 This is the **point** of the paragraph – it covers the first of the bullet points from the task.

2 This is the **evidence**, or detail, to support the point. Two sentences are used to give ideas about how money could be raised at the Ball.

3 This is the **explanation**. This explains how the evidence supports the point.

P.E.E. is a good structure to use when writing a text to persuade. Evidence like facts and statistics will help to make your points more believable and persuasive.

Sample answer

Formal Ball

One proposal is to hold one big event, such as a Formal Ball. Tickets could be sold, local companies could be asked to donate prizes for a large raffle and a local band could be persuaded to play free of charge. The local newspaper has shown an interest in taking photos, which could also be sold to raise funds. This could raise as much as £2,000, as well as generating a lot of useful publicity for the charity.

Now try this

Use P.E.E. to write up one more paragraph in answer to Task J from page 94.

Linking ideas

Your ideas can be linked together using adverbials. Adverbials help to guide the reader through your ideas.

Adding an idea

You can use the following adverbials to add another point/idea to your text.

In addition, ...

Additionally, ...

Furthermore, ...

Furthermore, litter is a danger to the health of the children who use the play area regularly.

Cause and effect

You can use the following adverbials to link causes to outcomes, effects and results in your text.

As a result, ...

Therefore, ...

Consequently, ...

Last year, we held a series of smaller fundraising events. **As a result**, everybody in the club was able to take part in at least one event.

Comparing and contrasting

You can use the following adverbials to compare and contrast similarities and differences in texts.

Comparing	Contrasting
Similarly, ...	However, ...
Likewise, ...	On the other hand, ...
In the same way, ...	On the contrary, ...

I understand that there is a need for more housing in the local area. **Likewise**, I appreciate the need to ensure young people are able to buy their first home. **However**, the Leisure Centre is a valued community facility ...

Notice how this student has used comparing and contrasting adverbials to introduce and dismiss a counter-argument.

Introducing evidence or developing a point

You can use the following adverbials to introduce evidence to your text.

For example, ...

For instance, ...

For example, 76% of people surveyed said they stayed away from local parks because of the litter.

Ordering points

You can use the following adverbials to organise your ideas into a logical order.

Firstly, ...

Secondly, ...

Next, ...

Finally, ...

Firstly, I would like to point out that the Leisure Centre is the only facility in the local area where people can obtain free fitness advice.

Now try this

Read the first paragraph of a student's answer for Task G (page 91) on the right. Add a range of adverbials to link the ideas and guide the reader through them logically.

You know you don't do enough exercise. You spend at least four hours of every day playing video games. You take the bus to work, even though it is less than a mile! You're at risk of heart disease and obesity.

Putting it into practice

You have now revised:

- planning your answer
- paragraphs
- Point–Evidence–Explain
- using adverbials.

Look at the extract from Task E below and see how a student has used structure to write their answer.

Task E

Write a letter to Ms Talia Albert, Head of Planning, Broxtown Council, 3 Oak Lane, Broxtown, BR2 5NG.

In your letter you should:

- state whether you agree or disagree with the Council's proposals
- give detailed reasons to support your views
- state clearly what action you want the Council to take.

Remember to write in sentences and use Standard English.

(15 marks)

Getting it right

For every writing task, make sure you:

✓ underline key words in the task about audience, purpose and format

✓ plan before you start writing

✓ use clear paragraphs

✓ develop all your points and use adverbials to signpost your ideas.

Sample answer

I am writing in response to your request for comments about the Council's proposal to demolish the Leisure Centre. I would like to explain why I completely disagree with this proposal.

The Leisure Centre is vital to the health of local residents. Research suggests that over 45% of adults in our town are overweight and at danger of developing serious health problems. The Leisure Centre is the only facility in the area to offer fitness advice free of charge. The Centre is a meeting place for families and young people. It is important for keeping young people off the streets.

✓ The student has included a clear introduction that uses details from the task.

✓ Clear topic sentence

✓ Use of P.E.E. to develop the idea

✗ The ideas have not been clearly signposted with adverbials.

✗ A new idea is introduced here so a new paragraph is needed.

✗ No evidence is given for this explanation.

✗ This student is attempting to argue a point about the Leisure Centre – the argument might be more effective if a counter-argument were given.

Now try this

Read the whole of Task E on page 89. Improve the second paragraph of the answer above.

- Use a new paragraph for each new idea.
- Use adverbials to signpost and link ideas.
- Use a counter-argument to make the writing more persuasive.

Vocabulary

Using a variety of vocabulary will make your writing more interesting.

Synonyms

Synonyms are words with similar meanings. Use them in your writing to avoid repetition and to add variety.

> You can find synonyms by looking up a word in the dictionary. Practise finding interesting alternatives to words you use often.

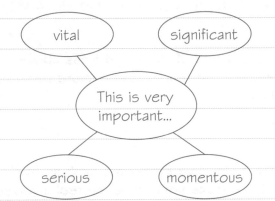

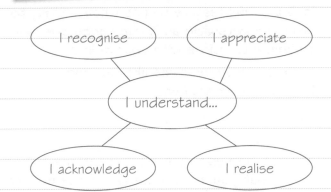

Vocabulary for impact

Using emotive language can add impact and interest to your writing.

Writers use emotive language to inform the reader of facts, while expressing positive or negative connotations. For example, read the three sentences below and look at the different impact each of the synonyms has:

Closing the Leisure Centre will be a **problem** for the whole community.

Closing the Leisure Centre will be a **catastrophe** for the whole community.

Closing the Leisure Centre will be a **game-changer** for the whole community.

Intensifying your vocabulary

Add even more power to your sentences by intensifying emotive vocabulary:

Closing the Leisure Centre will be a **terrible** disaster for the health of the whole community.

Closing the Leisure Centre will be a **monstrous** disaster for the health of the whole community.

Closing the Leisure Centre will be an **awful** disaster for the health of the whole community.

Now try this

Look at a student's paragraph for Task E on page 89. Replace the words and phrases in bold with more interesting vocabulary choices.

- Think about interesting synonyms.
- Think about using more emotive language.
- Think about intensifying any emotive vocabulary.

The Council must **understand** the effect the closure will have on the **health** of the local community. Closing the Leisure Centre will be an **issue** for everybody, but it will be particularly **important** for those who use it for health reasons.

Language techniques 1

You can use certain language features to add impact to your writing and to make it more suitable for its purpose.

Rhetorical questions

A **rhetorical question** doesn't require an answer, but it encourages readers to think about the topic themselves.

It is a useful feature to use when writing to argue or persuade as it can encourage your audience to agree with your points.

For example, questions like the one below have only one answer.

Do you want to become an unhealthy couch potato?

You can also use rhetorical questions to make what you are writing about seem more interesting or exciting.

Who wouldn't want to try Estrick's tastiest burger?

> Notice the use of emotive language to make this direct address more effective: 'menace' makes the litter sound like a serious threat.

Direct address

Talking **directly to the reader** can be very effective.

You will see the benefits after only a few days.

The example of direct address above involves the reader and is more persuasive than:

✗ There will be many benefits after a few days.

Using inclusive pronouns, such as 'we', can help to make your audience feel involved.

If we do nothing about the menace of litter, then nothing will change. It is up to all of us to act now.

Lists

You can use a list to:

• suggest you have a range of ideas

The Bistro has a huge variety of organic produce including seasonal vegetables, locally grown fruit and delicious British cheeses.

• add impact to your arguments.

Taking part in the detox will be simple, cheap, fun and great for your health.

Repetition

Repeating a word or phrase can emphasise a key point or idea in your writing.

Litter ruins parks for children. Litter ruins the countryside for ramblers. Litter ruins our rivers and kills our fish. It is time to take action.

Repetition is often most effective when a word or phrase is repeated three times. This adds rhythm and emphasis to your ideas.

Now try this

Read Tasks E and I on pages 89 and 93. Write **two** sentences for each task, using one of the techniques above in each sentence.

> When choosing language techniques, always make sure your vocabulary choices are appropriate for your audience.

Language techniques 2

You can use certain types of language to create images in your audience's minds. This is especially useful when writing to describe, but it can be effective in all types of writing.

Alliteration

Alliteration is the technique of using two or more words that start with the same sound. It can add rhythm and interest to your writing.

If you are thinking of visiting the Nature Reserve, you must stop at the café for one of the **truly tasty teas**.

Feeling **lazy, low** and **lost** without your phone? Come and join us on a jog!

Notice how alliteration is even more effective when combined with other techniques such as rhetorical questions and direct address.

Personification

Personification is the technique of attributing a human characteristic to something non-human. It is very effective when writing to describe.

Sunlight **danced** on the water of the boating lake.

The running bug **grabbed** me when I was only ten.

Personification helps readers to relate the actions of inanimate objects to their own emotions and experiences.

Similes

A **simile** is a figure of speech that involves suggesting a similarity or comparison between one thing and another.
For example:

For me, **running is as exhilarating as a skydive** from 30,000 feet.

The Olympic runner sprinted **like a cheetah**.

Don't try to force too many techniques into each piece of writing. Avoid using similes and metaphors that your audience will have read many times before, such as 'cool as a cucumber' or 'white as a sheet'.

Metaphors

A **metaphor** is a direct comparison suggesting a resemblance between one thing and another. It can be used:

• **to describe**

The café is the jewel in the crown of the Nature Reserve.

• **to argue or persuade.**

Litter is a scar on our town's landscape.

Getting it right

In the test, use different language techniques to add detail to your answer and make your writing interesting. Don't spend too long trying to think of lots of them!

Now try this

Read Tasks C and F on pages 87 and 90. Write **two** sentences for each task using one of the techniques above in each sentence.

Putting it into practice

You have now revised:

- choosing vocabulary for impact and effect
- using language techniques for impact and purpose.

Look at the test-style task below and read a student's answer.

Task F

Information

You read the notice on the right in the *Broxtown Local News*.

Writing task

Write an article for the *Broxtown Local News*, describing your life-changing moment in detail.

In your article you should:

- say when your life-changing moment happened
- describe the occasion or experience that was life-changing
- explain what made it life-changing for you.

Remember to write in sentences and use Standard English.

(15 marks)

Life-Changing Moments

We've all had one – a moment when your life changes forever. It might be the day you left school, the day you started a new job or just a day when you did something absolutely amazing. Perhaps you took on a challenge for charity, or finally achieved a lifetime goal.

Why don't you get in touch and tell our readers about your life-changing moment? Whether your story is inspiring or simply amusing, we would like you to share your moment with our readers. The best moments will be published in the paper every Monday.

Sample answer

My life-changing moment happened when I broke my leg jumping out of a tree. I was down the park with my mates and they dared me to climb this really tall tree. I was about eight. So I climbed up the tree. I got about a metre up and it felt like I was nearly at the sky. I was really scared and it was really cold. An arctic wind crept past my neck and I grabbed on really tightly.

Although there are some effective language choices here, there are also missed opportunities to use effective language.

✗ Language choice is too informal and lacks impact.

✗ Needs emotive language for effect.

✗ Repeated word 'climb' lacks impact.

✓ Effective use of a simile: 'like I was...'.

✗ The word 'really' is repeated but without creating impact.

✓ Effective use of a metaphor: 'arctic wind'.

✓ Effective use of personification: 'crept'.

Now try this

Re-read Task F above and rewrite the student's paragraph above by:

- replacing the informal language with language that has impact and is suitable for audience, format and purpose
- using emotive vocabulary for impact
- replacing the word 'climb' with more emotive vocabulary
- replacing the word 'really' with an appropriate synonym.

Sentences

For both your writing tasks you will need to write in complete and correct sentences. You should also use a variety of sentence lengths to add interest to your writing.

1 Simple sentences

Simple sentences make one point and have **one verb**. A **verb** is an action word. Every sentence needs a verb and somebody or something to 'do' the verb.

The Leisure Centre is closing.
⌐verb

2 Adding detail to simple sentences

You can add extra details to simple sentences, to show when, where or how the action is happening.

I am angry about the Council's proposals as I go by bike to the Leisure Centre every weekend.
          when   how   where

3 Linking simple sentences

To make your writing more interesting, you can put simple sentences together to make longer ones. You can do this by using linking words, such as:

- **and** to join two points or to add a point

We went to the zoo **and** we followed the nature trail.

We had chips in the café **and** a coffee.

- **or** to show alternatives to your point

Visitors can go to the zoo **or** follow the nature trail.

- **but** to add something that disagrees with your point

We had chips in the café, **but** I would rather have had cake.

- **because** to explain your point.

We had chips **because** I was very hungry.

4 Developing your sentences

You can develop your points within sentences by using adverbials, such as:

Litter is a serious issue in our town, **however** I do appreciate that it will be costly to deal with.

While I am in favour of having more litter collections, I feel the fast-food companies should bear some of the cost.

Although I do not use the Leisure Centre regularly, I know it is a life line for many people who need to lose weight.

The Bistro's menu has something for every member of the family, **for example** they even sell a range of organic baby food.

All our members will want to take part in fundraising activities, **therefore** running a variety of events is the best option.

Go to page 65 to revise using commas.

Now try this

Read the notes on the right from a student's plan for Task F on page 90. Write a paragraph aiming to use:

- at least **one** simple sentence
- **one** simple sentence with **when, where** or **how** detail added
- at least one longer sentence using a **linking** or **developing word**.

Life-changing event
First day at school, scared, big building, lots of people
Met best friend when sat together in assembly

Sentence variety

You can make your writing more interesting by using a variety of different sentence lengths and openings.

Sentence openings

Try to start your sentences in different ways. This will draw your reader in and make them want to read on. You can start with any of these:

* a pronoun, e.g.

  I, you, he, she, it, we, they, my, your, his, her, their

  We urgently need to address this problem ...

* a preposition, e.g. above, behind, between, near, with, on, under

  Above the restaurant is a well-equipped function room which can be hired for events such as weddings and parties.

* an 'ing' verb, e.g.

  running, hurrying, waiting, holding

  Holding a variety of fundraising events throughout the year ...

* an adjective (a describing word), e.g.

  slow, quiet, large, huge

  Huge puddings aren't usually my thing, but I made an exception for the Bistro's chocolate mousse.

* an adverb (a word that describes a verb), e.g.

  alarmingly, painfully, happily, quickly

  Alarmingly, the fast-food outlets on the high street do not seem concerned about the litter issue.

> If you use an adverb at the start of a sentence, remember to put a comma after it.

Sentence length

Varying sentence length prevents your writing from seeming monotonous.

Too many long sentences can make a text hard to read. And too many short sentences make a text sound choppy.

Using a mixture of sentence lengths means that you can grasp the reader's interest with short, catchy phrases, whilst developing details, points and ideas in longer sentences.

Go to page 59 to revise linking sentences.

Getting it right

In your test, think about the type of text you have been asked to write. In an informative article, you might need to link together complicated ideas using long sentences. In a speech you should mostly use short sentences because they are clear and easy to say.

Now try this

Read Task F on page 90. Using at least **three** of the above styles of sentence opener, write the first paragraph of an answer.

Writing about the present and future

Sentences can be about:

- what is happening now – the present tense
- what will happen in the future – the future tense
- what has already happened – the past tense.

What are verbs?

Verbs (doing words) can change when the tense changes.

Verbs can be:

Action verbs – what somebody or something is doing:

I visit the café every week.

Being verbs – what somebody or something is:

The Nature Reserve café is open on Sundays.

To write about the present or future you need to think about the verb in your sentence.

Present tense verbs

These examples will help you to revise how to use verbs in the present tense:

I visit the café every week.

He visits the Nature Reserve every Thursday.

They walk through the park every day.

She runs through the park in the morning.

The dog barks when she sees visitors.

We dance on Friday mornings.

Janet and Fred jog each evening.

I hate the cold, it makes me shiver.

Add an **s** to the end of a verb for **he, she, it** or **one name**.

Future tense verbs

When you write about the future you can use either of the following before the verb:

- **will**
- **going + to.**

The verb does not change when you add **will** before it, and it is the same for **I, you, he, she, it, they** and **we.**

I will walk to town tomorrow.

She will visit the Nature Reserve.

We will do a sponsored walk.

The verb before **going** is not the same for **I, you, he, she, it, they** and **we.**

Add **am** for **I**

Add **is** for **he, she, it** or **one name**

Add **are** for **you, we** or **they**

I am going to go to the park.

She is going to do a sponsored swim.

We are going to see the film.

> Notice that if you choose to write 'going', you need to add 'to' before the verb that follows.

Now try this

Select the correct verb in each of these sentences:

1. I wakes/wake up every day at 6 a.m. for work.
2. Ben are going/is going to take his mother to the Nature Reserve next year.
3. They will arrive/arrives at 5 p.m.
4. I love my new alarm clock; it wakes/wake me up very gently.

Writing about the past

To write about things that have already happened, you must use the past tense.

Past tense verbs

Like the present and future tenses, to write about the past you need to think about the verb in your sentence.

I watch**ed** a film.
She complain**ed** about the pens. — For most verbs, you add **ed** to the end to make them past tense.
He want**ed** to go swimming.

He hop**ed** to go to the seaside. — When verbs already end in **e**, just add **d** to the end.
Ben invit**ed** me to his party.

I **tried** hard to get home on time. — Verbs that end in **y** change to **ied**.
Ben **carried** his suitcase to work.
The children **cried** because they were hungry. — For some verbs, you have to double the final consonant (all letters other than vowels) before adding **ed**.

I trave**lled** a long way.
I sto**pped** eating chips.

Verbs with their own rules

Some verbs do not follow the rules above. You will need to learn these:

I do > I did	I take > I took	I know > I knew
I have > I had	I go > I went	I buy > I bought
I see > I saw	I make > I made	I bring > I brought
I eat > I ate	I come > I came	I sing > I sang
I get > I got	I sleep > I slept	

Unlike the present tense verbs, the past tense verbs in the table above don't change depending on who or what you are writing about. The verb **to be** is an exception and you are likely to use it often so you should learn it:

I am	>	I was
you are	>	you were
he/she/it is	>	he/she/it was
we are	>	we were
they are	>	they were

Notice that the past tense verbs for **I** and **he/she/it** are the same, and the past tense verbs for **you**, **we** and **they** are the same.

Now try this

Read this student's answer to Task I on page 93. Select the correct verb for the past tense.

We have/had a fantastic day at Burstone Nature Reserve! We followed/follows the nature trail for miles until we were/was tired out. Ben and I see/saw lots of different birds. Ben laughs/laughed as I copyed/copied the bird noises on the way round.

Putting it into practice

You have now revised:

- simple sentences
- adding detail to sentences
- varying your sentences
- writing in the past, present and future tenses.

Now, read the test-style task below and look at how a student has answered.

Task D

You decide to apply for a volunteering trip. Write your letter of application to: Lev Petrov, Venture Volunteering, 4 Forest Lane, Burstone, BG1 4HH.

In your letter you should:

- explain why you want to be a volunteer
- describe what type of charity project you would like to work on
- explain why you are suitable to be a volunteer.

Getting it right

When answering a writing task, remember to:

- read the question carefully
- underline the audience, purpose and format
- make a plan using the task bullet points and information.

Sample answer

I went to Vietnam during my gap year. I visit an orphanage and helpd out for a few days. This is interesting and worthwhile work. The orphanage was full of children with difficult backgrounds who are all still happy. My trip inspire me to apply for a volunteering job.

I have some skills which make me suitable for volunteering. I'm an excellent cook and have worked as a part-time chef in a local restaurant. I've also worked as an activity organiser on a camping site, which has given me valuable experience of entertaining children of all ages. I love working with people and feel I am very friendly and approachable.

✗ These verbs have not been correctly changed into the past tense.

✗ The tense changes here. The trip to Vietnam was in the past, so it would be better to write about it in the past tense in every sentence.

✗ This paragraph has a lot of short sentences. Some of them could be joined using linking words.

✓ This paragraph uses the correct tense throughout.

✗ This paragraph has been developed with detail, but all the sentences start with 'I'. Using different sentence openings would make it more interesting to read.

✗ Notice how the second paragraph contains two contractions. This is a letter of application meaning a formal style would be more appropriate.

Now try this

Always think about how formal or informal your writing needs to be.

Correct the student's paragraph above.

1 Make sure all the sentences use the correct tense.
2 Use linking words to join together some of the sentences in the first paragraph.
3 Use a variety of sentence openers to make the second paragraph more interesting to read.

Full stops and capital letters

Both your writing tasks will be marked for correct use of punctuation. Make sure you start each sentence with a capital letter. You must end your sentences with a full stop, an exclamation mark or a question mark.

Joining sentences

The most common mistake is joining two sentences with a comma instead of using a full stop.

If you are separating two pieces of information or two ideas, you should not use a comma:

✗ The Nature Reserve has many varieties of geese, visitors are not allowed to feed any of them.

You should use two separate sentences:

✓ The Nature Reserve has many varieties of geese. Visitors are not allowed to feed any of them.

Or you could join them with a conjunction:

✓ The Nature Reserve has many varieties of geese **but** visitors are not allowed to feed any of them.

Go back to page 59 to revise linking sentences.

Questions and exclamations

If you are writing a question, remember to end it with a question mark:

Why don't people recycle glass bottles?

If you want to show excitement or warn of danger, you can end your writing with an exclamation mark:

Our town even has an indoor ski slope!

Be careful when you use exclamation marks. Follow these rules:

• Don't use them too often.

• Never use two or more exclamation marks in a row.

Using capital letters

You should always use a capital letter to start a sentence. You should also use a capital letter at the start of:

• people's names, for example: Mr Malik, Lionel Messi, Mrs Jane Hughes

• names of places, for example: London, Barcelona, Paris

• the month in a date, for example: 20 January 2016.

Names, dates and addresses

Remember to use capital letters correctly for the name, address and date in a letter:

Jane Edwards

Head of the Environment Department

Estrick Council

Main Street

Estrick

ES1 3MS

20 January 2016

Now try this

Rewrite the following sentences. End one with a full stop, one with a question mark and one with an exclamation mark. Make sure you add any missing capital letters.

1 do you want your child hurt by these loose tiles

2 Jane smith suggested I send my complaint to you

3 don't hold a lit firework

Commas

You should use punctuation in your writing to help readers understand what you mean. Commas are useful for separating information within a sentence.

Commas to separate extra information

You can use commas to add extra detail to a sentence:

The Bistro, which is open every day of the week, offers a variety of special deals.

Sometimes the extra information can be put at the start of a sentence. When it is, you only need one comma:

As they are always popular, formal balls raise large sums of money.

Be careful – if the extra information comes after the main point of your sentence, there is no need for a comma:

Formal balls raise large sums of money as they are very popular.

> For more help, go back to page 59 to revise sentences.

Commas to join two points

Two sentences can be joined using a linking word and a comma. The comma is added before the joining word to create a pause between the two parts of the sentence:

I enjoyed my meal. I waited far too long for dessert.

I enjoyed my meal, but waited far too long for dessert.

The Leisure Centre is vital to the area's health, so it must remain open.

Be careful with commas. Don't use them to join two pieces of information unless you use a linking word.

> To check if you are using these commas correctly, remove the commas and the words inside them. If the sentence still makes sense, you're using them correctly.

Commas in a list

If you are writing a list, add a comma after each word or phrase.

You do not need a comma between the last two things. You can use 'and' or 'or'.

The Nature Reserve has birds, small mammals, rare duck breeds and many different varieties of geese.

To prove you are over 18 you will need a driving licence, a birth certificate or a passport.

Commas to introduce direct speech

Use a comma to introduce a quotation within a sentence.

Laura Buchanan explains, 'Managing your finances well is crucial to building a strong business.'

> Go to page 66 to revise inverted commas in quotations.

> **Now try this**

Correct or join these sentences by using commas:

1 I really wanted a hot meal but the Bistro is closed on Mondays.
2 A new hot food area need not be too costly. It would benefit all employees.
3 When the hot food area has been fitted employees will not need to leave the building at lunchtime.
4 We could consider adding a pizza oven a jacket potato oven a salad bar and a coffee machine.

Apostrophes and inverted commas

An apostrophe is used to show that a letter is missing, or to indicate possession. Inverted commas are used for quotations and titles, for example of films and books.

Inverted commas

Inverted commas can be either single (' ') or double (" "). They should always be used in pairs. Titles of things like films or books are often put inside inverted commas:

'The Adventures of Sherlock Holmes' are a terrific collection of books.

In 'Jog your way to Fitness', David Edwards explains how to jog without injury.

Inverted commas are also used when you quote something somebody else has said:

David Edwards explains, "A warm-up routine is vital, even before a short run."

You can use either single or double inverted commas for titles and speech, but you must use the same style throughout your writing.

Apostrophes for missing letters

When words are shortened, some letters are missed out. An apostrophe shows where letters are missing:

cannot ⟶ can't

do not ⟶ don't

I will ⟶ I'll

let us ⟶ let's

Words that are shortened like this are called **contractions**. They are more informal than the full form. Think carefully about your audience when deciding which to use.

Go back to pages 46 and 47 to revise formal and informal writing.

Apostrophes of possession

Apostrophes are also used to show that something or someone belongs to someone or something else.

The apostrophe goes between the owner and the 's':

The boy's hands

Betty's sister

The dog's collar

The school's head teacher

Apostrophe warning!

'It's' means 'it is'. The apostrophe shows the letter 'i' is missing.

It's very cold at the Nature Reserve in the winter.

This replaces the missing letter 'i'.

'Its' means belonging to someone or something. To make sure it is not confused with the contraction for 'it is', there is no apostrophe.

The company opened its fourth shop last year.

This shows that the shop belongs to the company.

Now try this

Correct these sentences by adding apostrophes or inverted commas.

1 Barbaras Bistro is simply the best in town.
2 Its best to visit the Nature Reserve in the summer.
3 When I visited the Reserve, I took the book 101 British Birds with me.
4 This restaurants burgers are the biggest in town, another diner assured me.

Spelling tips

Both your writing tasks are marked for spelling. You can use a dictionary in the test to check spellings, but this will use up a lot of time if you do it too often.

 ## The i before e rule

As **i** and **e** often appear together, it can be difficult to remember which comes first. Use the **i before e rule** to help you remember:

i before e except after c, but only when it rhymes with bee

believe

rhymes with bee, so i goes **before e**

receive

rhymes with bee but comes **after the c**, so **e** goes **before i**

eight

doesn't rhyme with bee, so e goes **before i**

science

comes after c, but it **doesn't rhyme with bee**, so i goes **before e**

 ## Ly or ley?

When you add **-ly** to a word ending with **e**, make sure you don't swap the **l** and the **e**. For example:

definite + ly = definitely

bravley ✗   bravely ✓

safley ✗   safely ✓

rudley ✗   rudely ✓

sincerley ✗   sincerely ✓

Make a note of the correct spelling of 'sincerely'. You might have to write a letter for one of your writing tasks. 'Yours sincerely' is one of the ways to end a formal letter.

> A few words don't follow the rules: weird, seize, caffeine, species. Practise looking up unfamiliar **ie** or **ei** words in a dictionary before your test.

 ## Words with double letters

Words with double letters can be difficult to spell, as you can't hear the double letters when you say the word. Learn how to spell these words:

address	necessary	tomorrow
different	possible	professional
immediately	occasionally	success
eventually	possible	beginning
opportunity	difficult	recommend
disappoint	disappear	
embarrassing	possession	

 ## Silent letters

Some words have letters that you can't hear when you say the word.

These are some words with silent letters:

when	which	whole
could	knife	autumn
climb	Wednesday	sign
listen	wrong	talk

> When you think a word has a double letter, check it in the dictionary. Learn which letters in the word are doubled and which are not.

Now try this

Correct the mistakes in the following sentences:

1 Every paying visitor to the Nature Reserve recieves a reciept.
2 My mother told me to visit the Nature Reserve as it has lovley views.
3 Wen I get to the house, I cud suprise my mother.

Common spelling errors 1

Some common spelling errors are made with words that sound the same but are spelt differently.

 Their, there, they're

Their means belonging to them:

Their football boots are muddy.

There is used to explain the position of something:

The football boots were over there.

Or to introduce a sentence:

There is a place for muddy boots outside.

They're is a contraction of **they are**:

They're all tired after the football game.

 We're, wear, were and where

We're is a contraction of **we are**:

We're going to Spain.

Wear is a verb (doing word) that refers to clothing:

You need to wear a uniform at our school.

Were is the past tense of **are**:

They were late getting to the airport.

Where refers to place:

Where are we going?

 Your, you're

Your means belonging to you.

You're is a contraction of **you are**.

✗ Your having the time of you're life

✓ You're having the time of your life.

 To, too, two

To indicates place, direction or position:

I went to Spain.

Too means 'also', or a large amount:

I went too far.

Two is a number:

Two of us went to Spain last year.

 Of, off

The easiest way to remember the difference is by listening to the sound of the word you want to use:

- **of** is pronounced 'ov'
- **off** rhymes with 'cough'

✗ He jumped of the top off the wall.

✓ He jumped off the top of the wall.

 Are, our

Are is a verb (doing word):

We are going to the airport.

Our means belonging to us:

Our football boots are very muddy.

Remember that **a lot** is two words: A lot of people went to Spain.

Now try this

Select the correct spelling in these sentences:
1 The boots are two/to/too muddy to go in the car.
2 You are/our lucky to be going on holiday.
3 Students should take their/they're/there books to each lesson.
4 The plane takes off/of in an hour.
5 Your/You're going to love the film.

Common spelling errors 2

Some words are often used incorrectly.

 Would have, could have, should have

Students often make mistakes in the phrases **would have**, **could have** and **should have**. For example:

✗ Accidents could of been prevented. We should of fixed the pavement as soon as the cracks appeared.

✓ Accidents could have been prevented. We should have fixed the pavement as soon as the cracks appeared.

To help you remember, try reading the sentences without 'would', 'could' and 'should'. 'Accidents **have** been prevented' makes sense but the sentence would not make sense with 'of'.

 Bought or brought?

Bought and **brought** mean different things.

Bought is the past tense of **buy**:

Ravi bought an umbrella in the shop.

This means Ravi paid money for an umbrella.

Brought is the past tense of **bring**:

Ravi brought an umbrella in her bag.

This means Ravi was carrying an umbrella with her.

 Write or right

Write and **right** mean different things.

Write means to put something in writing, using a pen or pencil:

I need to write a shopping list.

Right is the opposite of **wrong**:

I need to know the right spelling for difficult words.

④ Know, now and no

Know means to have knowledge:

I know enough to pass my test.

Now means at the present time:

I now know enough to pass my test.

No is the opposite of **yes**:

'No! That spelling is not correct!'

Now try this

Cross out the incorrect word in these sentences:
1 With my new pen I can right/write in the write/right style.
2 I now/know I should of/should have looked where I was going.
3 I could have/could of bought/brought it cheaper at another shop.
4 The new mobile I brought/bought from Estrick Electronics is faulty.

Common spelling errors 3

Some of the most commonly misspelt words are listed below.

Commonly misspelled words

actually	conclusion	health	persuasion
although	decide	heart	physical
argument	decision	interrupt	preparation
atmosphere	definite	marriage	queue
audience	environment	meanwhile	remember
autumn	explanation	modern	secondary
beautiful	February	nervous	separate
because	fierce	performance	straight
business	guard	permanent	survey
caught	happened	persuade	unfortunately

 Learn correct spellings

Get into the habit of looking up new or unfamiliar words in a dictionary before your test. Then practise the correct spelling. You could use the look/cover/write/check method:

1. Look at the word.   2. Write it from memory.

3. Cover the word.   4. Check your spelling.

 Find hidden words

For example, **separate** becomes much easier to spell if you remember there is 'a rat' inside it: sep-a-**rat**-e

 What you see

Say the word aloud, breaking it into smaller parts. For example, say these words aloud to help you with the correct spelling:

def / in / ite / ly

fri / end

Wed / nes / day

Getting it right

If some of these words are unfamiliar, look them up in a dictionary. That way you will be building up your vocabulary for the test!

Go back to page 34 for tips on how to use a dictionary.

Now try this

Spend some time learning these spellings before your test. Test yourself and learn any you get wrong. You could ask somebody to help by testing you.

Plurals

Read these rules carefully; they explain the rules for making words into plurals.

Adding s

Most words can be made into plurals by adding **s**:

one test > two tests

a student > lots of students

If a word ends in **ch, sh, x, s** or **ss**, add **es** to make it plural:

one church   two churches

one splash   two splashes

one fox   two foxes

one bus   two buses

one glass   two glasses

Words that end in f or fe

To make a plural when a word ends in **f** or **fe**:

• change the **f** or **fe** to **v**

• add **es**.

loaf   loaves

half   halves

knife   knives

life   lives

Words that end in y

There are different rules for words **ending in y**, depending on the letter **before the y**.

If a word has a **vowel** (a, e, i, o, u) before the **y**, just **add s**:

toys   days   bays

trays   boys   keys

If a word has a **consonant** (any letter that is not a vowel) before the **y**, remove the **y** and add **ies**.

baby   babies

fly   flies

city   cities

Exceptions

Some words use a **different word** as their plural:

woman   women

man   men

foot   feet

tooth   teeth

child   children

person   people

mouse   mice

Some words **don't change** when they are plural:

fish

sheep

deer

Learn these exceptions before your test.

Now try this

Write out the following sentences and cross out the incorrect words.

1 For the partys/parties, we need fourteen loafs/loaves of bread.

2 All the torchs/torches need new batteries/batterys.

3 A family ticket covers two adults and up to three childs/children on all buss/buses.

4 Men/Mans are just as clever as womans/women.

Checking your work

It is important to leave time at the end of your writing tasks to check your work. Follow these steps to make sure you find any mistakes in your writing.

Careful checking

Always check your work carefully. It is a good idea to check it three times:

- once for spelling
- once for punctuation
- once to check it makes clear sense with no misused, repeated or missing words.

When checking your answers, look for words, punctuation and grammar that you struggle with and focus your attention on these.

Checking for sense

1 When you check for sense, try to read aloud in your head. Imagine you can hear your voice. Does the work still make sense?

2 Remember to leave time to read through your work. Finish both writing tasks before checking, then go back to Task 1.

3 If you come across a sentence that doesn't make sense, read it again. Then think about what you can do to put it right.

Know your strengths

When you are preparing for your test and answering past test questions, you should identify which things you can do well and which things you find difficult. What kinds of mistake do you make:

- spelling mistakes?
- missing or incorrect punctuation?
- missing words?
- using the wrong word?

Alarm bells

Train yourself to hear alarm bells when you come across tricky words, such as:

- their/there/they're
- its/it's
- your/you're.

Stop when you come to any of these words. Double check that you have used the correct spelling for the meaning you intended.

Putting it right

If you find a mistake – cross it out. Put ~~one neat line through the mistake~~ and add your correction:

- either by using an arrow (→) to the new words to guide the reader
- or by using an asterisk (*) *to tell the reader to read this bit next.

Getting it right

Leaving a brief break before checking your work in the test will help to improve your focus.

Now try this

Look at your answer to the task on page 58. Follow the tips above on checking for sense. When you find mistakes, correct them using the **Putting it right** methods above.

Putting it into practice

You have revised:

- punctuation
- spelling
- checking your work.

Now look at the test-style task below and see how one student has answered.

Task J

Write the report for the club committee meeting. In your report you should:

- explain the benefits of holding one large fundraising event
- explain the benefits of holding several smaller fundraising events
- suggest which you think would be best for the club.

(15 marks)

Getting it right

Check your work carefully. It is a good idea to check through your work three times:

- once for spelling
- once for punctuation
- once to check it makes clear sense with no misused, repeated or missing words.

Sample answer

Fundraising Report

One main fundraising event

charlotte our club secretary has suggested that we hold just one fundriasing event per year. This could be a formale ball, as they are always very popular with all of our players. We coud charge for tickets and we could have a raffle an auction and a sale of Club jackets. Holding a ball would be better for those of you who are players who are not able to help out. If we have the ball in febuary we wuld be able too hyer the councils community hall very cheaply.

A disadvantige of holding a ball is that we'd have to spend alot on advertising to perswade enouf people to come.

✗ some wrong words have been used

✗ many spelling mistakes

✗ missing commas in a list

✗ comma missing for extra detail

✗ capital letters missed

✗ second paragraph lacks detail

✓ An apostrophe has correctly been used to shorten 'we would' into 'we'd'. However, a report is a formal text, so the language should be formal: 'we would' is more suitable than 'we'd'.

Now try this

Rewrite the student's answer:

- correcting all the style, spelling and punctuation mistakes
- adding more detail about the disadvantages of holding a ball.

73

Putting it into practice (example answer)

Look at a student's answer to Task D on page 88, below. Read the comments to see why this is a good answer.

Sample answer

> 4 New Street
> Broxtown
> BS1 2JY
>
> Lev Petrov,
> Venture Volunteering,
> 4 Forest Lane,
> Burstone,
> BG1 4HH   12th May 2016
>
> Dear Mr Petrov
>
> I am writing to apply for the opportunity to take part in one of your volunteering trips.
>
> I have a passion for visiting different countries. Recently, I visited Vietnam and was lucky enough to visit an orphanage run entirely by volunteers. Many of them told me how rewarding they find the work. This visit inspired me to spend my next holiday working as a volunteer.
>
> I would really like the opportunity to work on an educational project. I have just finished my education and know how valuable it will be to my future.
>
> I've spent the last two summers working as an activity assistant at a local play centre. This involved planning childrens parties, supervising them while they used the equipment and serving them meals in the café. While I have no teaching qualifications, this work has given me some experience of working with children.
>
> I'm hard-working, enthusiastic and freindly. I look forward to hearing from you.
>
> Yours sincerely,
> Jane Smith

What has been done well:

✓ Format is correct for a letter. It has two addresses in the right places, a date and the correct opening and closing.

✓ The bullet points from the question have been used to structure the answer.

✓ The style is mostly formal, which suits the audience and purpose.

✓ The student has used clear P.E.E. structure to organise two of the paragraphs.

✓ Spelling is mostly accurate, with only one mistake (in the last paragraph). There is some interesting vocabulary.

✓ Punctuation is accurate except for one missing apostrophe; the student has used commas correctly.

✓ Grammar is correct, with some varied sentences and different sentence openers. The tense is correct throughout.

What could be improved:

✗ Some of the sentences in the second paragraph could be linked and the word 'visit' replaced by more interesting vocabulary.

✗ The third paragraph is a little brief. Some detail about why education is valuable could be added.

✗ The style should be formal all the way through. Towards the end, contractions have been used.

✗ There is a spelling mistake and some punctuation errors.

Now try this

Use this answer to help you revise.

- Find the spelling and punctuation errors and correct them.
- Rewrite the second paragraph, linking some of the sentences and replacing the word 'visit' with more interesting vocabulary.
- Rewrite the third paragraph, adding more detail about why education is valuable.

Putting it into practice (example answer)

Look at a student's answer to Task I on page 93, below. Read the comments to see how this answer could be improved.

Sample answer

<u>Burstone nature reserve</u>

Burstone nature reserve opened last September and is a good place for you to take your kids.

I goes there a lot, as they have a large selection of small animals wich the kids can hold. Are kids love the nature trial and always listen too the experiensed giuide's. The reserve has alot of rare bird's, geese and swan's on the boating lake and you can hyer a boat and row around on a sunny afternoon.

I enjoy the café best of all. They have the best cream cakes and I love the gift shop as it has lots of toys the kids like.

Go soon, its great!

Getting it right

Always plan before you write. This student has failed due to lack of planning, as the review is not logically structured. Checking at the end is also important. Always read through your work to make sure it makes sense.

Go back to page 49 to revise planning.

What has been done well:

✓ The student has used the correct format for a review, with a clear title.

✓ The student has used paragraphs.

✓ The student has tried to use a variety of sentences.

✓ Full stops and an exclamation mark have been used.

✓ Commas have been used for a list.

✓ The student has included some detail.

What could be improved:

✗ The title could be more interesting and give some idea of the writer's opinion.

✗ The review mentions who uses it and why, but is not structured using the bullet points. One paragraph should describe the attractions and one should explain what was enjoyable. Instead, there is too much information in the second paragraph and none of the points is developed with detail. This means the review is too short.

✗ More descriptive detail is needed to make the Reserve sound exciting. Similies or personification could be used to describe the attractions.

✗ One of the sentences in the third paragraph contains two different ideas, so it should be two separate sentences.

✗ There are mistakes in grammar and too many spelling errors. Words that appear in the task information should always be copied accurately.

✗ Some punctuation is missing.

Now try this

Use the answer above to help you revise. Rewrite the review, making the improvements suggested above.

Remember to make varied vocabulary choices to keep your writing original and interesting.

TEXT A

The article below talks about addiction to technology and its negative effects.

ARE WE ALL ADDICTS?

Picture the scene. A typical family are about to sit down for a tasty home-cooked meal after a hard day at school and work. The eldest daughter pours the water, the youngest puts out the knives and forks and the son puts a large bowl into the centre of the table. A healthy salad, you're probably thinking. Wrong.

The bowl in the middle of the table contains all the family's mobile technology, and is part of an experiment by Mersey University into the effect of technology on our lives. Ten families have been asked to limit their use of technology to just two hours a day. But calling two hours a 'limit' seems surprising. Does anybody really spend that much time glued to their phone?

It seems they do. According to research by the communications watchdog Comwatch, we spend more than 27 hours a week on the internet. Young people aged 14 to 18 spend a staggering 60 hours a week using technology such as phones and tablets. That means young people are spending half their lives staring at a screen. When do they have time to do their homework, be with their families or play sport? Let alone sleep!

I see myself as a bit of a dinosaur where technology is concerned. I was convinced that a quick check-up of my screen time would reveal me to be way below average. Oh dear. I was online for over 30 minutes before even eating my breakfast. I have to confess that I stop working several times an hour to have a crafty look at my text messages. Given that I can easily spend an hour browsing online while watching TV in the evening, I am beginning to worry that I am, in fact, an online junkie.

This addiction to the online world comes at a cost. It disrupts our sleep, prevents face-to-face communication and is turning us into couch potatoes.

So how are the ten families adapting to the reduction in technology time? Remarkably well, according to Professor Jess Smithers of the university research team. "It's early days, but so far all our families seem to be adjusting well. We are getting reports of way more quality family time and several people have recorded an improvement in their sleep patterns."

TEXT B

> The poster below offers advice for mastering technology and using it wisely.

WHO'S THE SLAVE? MASTERING THE ONLINE WORLD

With so much technology at our fingertips these days, it is easier than ever to waste hours watching funny videos of cats. Many people feel they have become slaves to their devices, checking their messages, reading the news and flicking through social media throughout the day for fear of missing out.

So, how do we use technology wisely? How do we become masters of the online world, rather than being its servants? Here are six top tips:

1. **Use it to save money** Many retailers post offers and vouchers on social networking sites, so 'Like' your favourite shops to stay up to date with the best deals. You can also cut down on your phone bill by messaging your friends through social media instead of using texts and phone calls.

2. **Learn a new skill or language** There are loads of free apps out there that can help you learn anything from Spanish, to DIY skills, to baking.

3. **Use online banking services** Nowadays, there is no need to visit a bank to make payments or find out your account balance. Most major banks now provide safe and easy-to-use online banking services to help you keep track of your finances on the go.

4. **Research anything and everything** The internet brings the world to your fingertips, so do something useful with it! You can use it to plan your next holiday, find somewhere new to eat lunch or help your children do their homework.

5. **Limit your time online** Slouching over your phone or computer all day can lead to back pain and poor posture. Put aside an hour a day to answer emails and texts, then go out and do something active!

6. **Stay safe** Never reveal your bank security details or other passwords. You should also make sure you have anti-virus software installed on your devices.

TEXT C

This article describes some of the benefits of technology for young people.

TECHNOLOGY – THE DIGITAL AWARENESS GENERATION

Are you dismayed by the amount of time young people spend on their phones and tablets? Do you criticise technology as a complete waste of time for children?

It may be time to stop moaning, as screen time may actually help to improve children's development.

A new study found that using interactive technology can help develop hand–eye coordination. Computer games where children have to follow the action onscreen while using the mouse were found to be excellent preparation for writing and using tools such as scissors.

Computer games are also excellent for developing attention span. You might find your child's complete absorption in a game frustrating, but a study of 100 children found that 75% of regular gamers had a longer attention span than children who never played online.

Active screen time also helps children develop language skills. By reading e-books and accessing stories online, they increase their vocabulary. Surprisingly, social networking sites can also be good for communication skills, giving young people the chance to express themselves creatively.

What children read online can also be helpful. There is no doubt that inappropriate content exists online, but there are also many excellent sources of advice especially for young people about issues such as relationships, wellbeing and health. And there is no better resource for researching homework or other interests.

Thanks to modern technology, there is a whole world of development and learning at every child's fingertips. But a word of warning – studies show that limiting screen time is essential. Sitting down for long periods is not good at any age, and even the most techno-savvy child needs fresh air every day!

TEXT D

The article below describes our consumption of gas and electricity, and its impact on our wallets.

A FUEL CRISIS?

The average UK family spends over £150 a month on electricity and gas to power and heat their homes. A new report into fuel usage reveals that for some lower-income families, fuel payments account for up to 20% of their total household income. Rent or mortgage payments can often represent half of a family budget, so having to spend nearly half of their remaining income on fuel causes real hardship.

According to a leading debt charity, this squeeze on UK household budgets has reached crisis point. Last year there was a dramatic rise in the number of people unable to pay their fuel bills, and the average amount owed in gas and electricity is over £2,000. Among pensioners over 70, the average is £500, meaning that some older people owe nearly five times the amount of their weekly state pension.

However, it is all too easy to blame rising fuel prices. Around a third of the fuel we pay for is wasted, mainly through inefficient or careless use of household appliances. We leave our TVs on standby, charge our phones and laptops overnight and light our houses as if it was Christmas all year round. We expect our homes to always be warm, so many of us have our heating switched on day and night.

Switching energy supplier is a good way to make savings on your fuel bills, and according to the Committee of Fuel Efficiency, consumers have already saved £2 million by switching suppliers. But chairman Stephen Chapman insists there is more we can do: 'We are still wasting fuel. Putting on a jumper and turning the heating down could halve our winter bills.'

He warns that we will not achieve any significant savings until we learn to value the fuel we pay for. 'We hear a lot about living in a throwaway society, but how many of us realise that the stuff we throw away includes fuel?'

TEXT E

> This leaflet details some ways we can reduce our consumption of energy.

QUICK ENERGY WINS

We all think we know how to keep our electricity and gas bills to a minimum. We've turned the thermostat down. We've checked out the most competitive tariff for our family and lifestyle. Now we can relax and enjoy our cosily heated homes, can't we?

Wrong. Fuel waste is a massive problem in the UK. Not only does it cause debt misery for millions who struggle to pay their bills, but it also damages the environment. Just a few simple steps can significantly reduce the fuel we waste in our homes, keeping bills low and reducing our impact on the planet.

What you can do:

1. Stop using standby mode. Teenagers are often the worst offenders here. Up to £80 a year can be saved just by getting them to switch their TVs and games consoles off at the socket.

2. Turn off lights. All it takes is the flick of a switch as you leave the room. Leaving a standard 60 watt bulb on all day will cost you about 10 pence; it doesn't sound like much but over a year it adds up.

3. Manage the temperature in each room. At any one time, half the rooms in your house could be sitting empty with the radiators on full blast. Install controllable valves on every radiator, and encourage teenagers to take responsibility for their room.

4. Insulate your loft. Half your heat can disappear through a loft that is not insulated. If you have recently moved, it is worth checking that your insulation is up to the latest government standards. Register to have it checked for free at www.saveyourenergy.com.

5. Check doors and windows for draughts. If your old windows are allowing valuable heat to escape, consider replacing them. Alternatively, fit draught-exclusion material and hang heavy curtains that drape onto the floor.

6. Consider solar panels. They can be expensive to fit, but government grants are available to help. Collecting your own energy from the sun will significantly reduce your bills, and you may even make a profit selling spare energy to the National Grid.

TEXT F

The article below questions whether we are all doing our bit to reduce gas and electricity use.

THE FUEL CRISIS – ARE WE ALL IN IT TOGETHER?

We have all heard about the fuel crisis. We're urged to turn our heating down. We're nagged to turn our lights off. We're assured that this will save us money and help the environment. But does sitting in a coat with the lights out actually make a real difference?

It seems it does. As a nation, domestic usage (and therefore wastage) of gas and electricity actually *dropped* in 2013 and is predicted to continue dropping at a rate of 0.5% every year for the next five years.

But this is not enough. According to Lily Xiao, Chairman of the World Energy Trust, we will exhaust our supply of fossil fuels before the end of this century unless we take drastic action to reduce our fuel waste. 'The irresponsible way we use fuel is not sustainable; if we do not act now it will be too late.'

However, evidence suggests that government departments and public services are exhausting these supplies faster than the general public. While nobody is suggesting that hospitals start turning down the heating and issuing more blankets, it is shocking that public organisations such as schools, libraries and councils do not take fuel saving seriously.

My children's school, for example, is an impressive new building with carefully controlled heating and lighting that switches off automatically. But it still relies solely on gas and electricity for its energy. The school faces south and has a beautiful expanse of smooth sloping roof tiles. Surely this would be a perfect site for solar panels?

Similarly, my local museum has recently been renovated at a cost of £5.3 million, but no thought was given to providing green energy. The shape of the building is not suitable for solar panels, but it sits on top of a hill surrounded by open fields, the ideal spot for a mini wind farm. Nowadays wind turbines are not that expensive to install either.

So – next time you're in a public building, make a nuisance of yourself. Find somebody in charge and ask them why they're not following the example of the general public and doing something about the fuel crisis.

TEXT G

This article details some of the problems with giving money to people begging on the street.

BEGGING – TO GIVE OR NOT TO GIVE?

Begging is illegal under the Vagrancy Act of 1824. However, it is not well enforced in many cities. Karim Akhtar, the Chief Constable of Broxtown Police Force, is determined to change this in his city. 'In response to concerns from the public, arrests for begging have increased by 50% over the past two years,' he stated.

Begging is not just a problem in big cities, either. Knoswick is a pretty town in the Estrick Hills that thrives on tourism. But begging is on the increase. 'It's our job to look our best. I worry what visitors think of the town, and how it will affect my business,' said hotel owner Nigel Shrike. Tourists who give money on the street encourage begging, and could ultimately be damaging local livelihoods.

You may think you're helping by giving to someone on the street, but you can't be sure that your money will be spent on essentials of life, such as food, clothing or shelter. Substance abuse is a common problem in the homeless community, so your kindness could do more harm than good. It's much more constructive to donate to a shelter, soup kitchen or homeless charity, where your money will fund proper care.

Not all beggars are genuine. There is evidence to suggest that organised gangs may be running begging scams in some cities. Police have found 'professional' beggars working in Broxtown and Estrick, where their earnings are as high as £100 each per day. Orla Duffy of Estrick Council said, 'We take gang activities very seriously, and are working with the police to tackle the problem.'

So think next time you are tempted to give. A handful of coins may seem like a quick and easy way to help, but you cannot be sure who your money is going to or how it will be spent, and in the long term you could be damaging the local community.

TEXT H

The report below describes the problem of homelessness for young people.

MISERY RISES FOR THE YOUNG

Government figures for the number of young people who are homeless are wildly inaccurate, according to research undertaken by a leading university.

The survey suggests that over 85,000 16- to 25-year-olds were homeless in 2014. This is over three times the number stated in the Government's official figures. The research calls the levels of homelessness 'a crisis', particularly as many young people are resorting to begging in order to feed themselves. It also claims that the situation may be even worse than the figures suggest, as they do not include those who are temporarily housed in shelters.

Many young people are not legally defined as homeless. A large number spend only a couple of nights a week actually sleeping rough, with other nights spent 'sofa-surfing' or sleeping in hostels. This means that local authorities do not have any legal obligation to house them.

Breakdown of relationships, usually between young people and their families or carers, is the most common cause of homelessness in this age group. This could start out as sleeping rough the occasional night after an argument, but can soon develop into a situation where they are without a home. In 2013, a charity survey found that around 7 in 10 young people seeking support with housing issues had left home due to poor family relationships.

Living on the streets often goes hand in hand with other serious issues. Many young homeless people suffer from mental health issues, which they have to handle alone without proper treatment or support. And without a permanent address, they are unable to apply for work or benefits, adding further stress and forcing them to beg or steal to survive.

The university survey puts forward several ideas for dealing with the crisis. These include changing the rules for local authority housing so that sleeping rough one night a week is enough to qualify as being homeless. It also suggests that police should prioritise helping young people on the streets find a safe place to sleep, rather than arresting them for begging.

TEXT I

> The advertisement below describes how you can help the homeless all year round.

HOMELESS HAVEN

Homeless Haven provides food, housing, support and friendship for the homeless across the UK. We transform the lives of vulnerable people, by providing somewhere safe and comfortable to stay and by helping them get back on their feet.

Why should you volunteer?

Volunteering allows you to give something back to your community and help people who are less fortunate than you. Many of our clients are under 25, so it's a good opportunity to work with young people and help them secure a brighter future.

What volunteering opportunities are available?

If you are interested in making a difference, Homeless Haven offers a range of volunteering opportunities to choose from.

Support Assistant	Provide care and support for our guests by welcoming and advising them, and looking after their welfare throughout their stay.
Kitchen Assistant	Work with our kitchen team to prepare tasty and healthy meals. Or if you prefer, work front-of-house and serve guests, help to clear tables and wash up after meals.
Outreach	Homeless people are often isolated and unaware of the shelter and the help we provide. Get out on the streets with our team and reach out to vulnerable young people when they need us the most.
Fundraising Assistant	Collecting money is one of our most important volunteering roles, and it takes place outside all year round in all weathers. No real skill is required to rattle a tin outside your local supermarket, but the money given to us in this way is vital. If you can't spare the time to volunteer with us, then pop your loose change into one of our tins.

When are volunteers needed most?

Christmas Day is the most popular shift and opportunities are often filled weeks in advance. However, like many other charities, we need angels all through the year to fill our night-shift slots. Sacrificing a night's sleep, whether as a one-off or on a regular basis, would be a real help in our fight to keep our night shelters open.

How can you volunteer?

We are looking for volunteers who are able to commit at least a day per week. If this applies to you, come and see us to find out how you can become part of our team and make a difference to vulnerable people's lives. We are open 24/7.

TASK A

INFORMATION
You read the following advert on a social networking site.

Community Funding needs your help!

We need help in the following areas:

- running stalls at weekly bring-and-buy sales
- delivering leaflets locally to advertise our fundraising events
- competing at our sponsored swimming and running events
- serving refreshments at our events
- acting as fundraising treasurer.

All money raised goes to local causes. So far, we have bought the kit for the local boys' football team and paid for the community centre to be re-decorated.

Any skills or previous experience would be very welcome but are not essential. If you have enthusiasm and spare time we will find something for you to do!

If you are interested, write an email to sylvie@communityfunds.net

 Like    Comment   Share

WRITING TASK
Write an email to Sylvie, offering to help in one or more areas.

In your email you should:
- identify any areas that interest you and explain why
- describe what qualities you have that make you suitable to help with fundraising.

You may include any other information.

Remember to write in sentences and use Standard English.

(15 marks)

TASK B

INFORMATION

Lately there has been a problem with people leaving litter in your local park. You decide to write an article about it for your school/college/community newsletter.

You make the following notes:

- most litter is soft-drink cans and fast-food containers
- spoils lovely community area for everybody
- litter is a health risk
- costs local councils millions of pounds a year to clear up
- litter is a hazard on pavements
- litter is a serious danger to wildlife in parks and nature spots.

WRITING TASK

Write an article for your school/college/community newsletter.

In your article you may:

- describe the issue of litter in your local park
- explain why it is a problem
- state what you think should be done about it.

You may include any other ideas.

Remember to write in sentences and use Standard English.

(15 marks)

TASK C

INFORMATION

You read the following advertisement in the *Burstone Weekly*, a community newspaper.

Now opened under new management: a terrific addition to Burstone's lively restaurant scene. An informal yet stylish destination, serving a delicious variety of food.

- All ingredients sourced from local organic producers

- Gluten-free menu options

- Large selection of local cheeses

- Jazz band on Thursday and Friday evenings

- Mid-week two for the price of one specials

Bring this advertisement to get an additional 25% off all food and drink on any Monday, Tuesday or Wednesday evening.

Come along any weekday lunchtime and sample our taster menu.

Children's play area open in the summer months.

WRITING TASK

When you visited the restaurant you were pleased with most aspects of it, but there were some problems. You decide to write a review of the restaurant for *Burstone Weekly*.

In your review you should:

- state what was good about the restaurant
- describe what the problems were
- suggest what improvements could be made.

Remember to write in sentences and use Standard English.

(15 marks)

TASK D

INFORMATION

You read the following advertisement in your local newspaper:

Volunteering opportunities!

Venture Volunteering has been running volunteering trips to many destinations worldwide since 1999.

Whatever your skill or interest, Venture Volunteering will have the perfect opportunity for you. We work alongside local charities that specialise in education, water and medical projects. Don't worry if you have no specialist skills – volunteers are always needed to help out in schools, reading to children, playing sports with them or serving their meals. If you are energetic, fit and enthusiastic you can spend your time outside helping to build a medical centre or vaccination clinic.

If you want to spend your next holiday doing something more rewarding than taking selfies, apply to join one of our trips.

WRITING TASK

You decide to apply for a volunteering trip. Write your letter of application to: Lev Petrov, Venture Volunteering, 4 Forest Lane, Burstone, BG1 4HH.

In your letter you should:

- explain why you want to be a volunteer
- describe what type of charity project you would like to work on
- explain why you are suitable to be a volunteer.

Remember to write in sentences and use Standard English.

(15 marks)

TASK E

INFORMATION

You read the following on your local council's noticeboard.

●● **Broxtown**
●● Council

Broxtown Leisure Centre to be closed

Broxtown Council regrets to announce that
it can no longer afford to maintain its Lakeside
Leisure Centre. A recent inspection has
highlighted several serious health and safety issues
that mean the building itself is unsafe.

The Leisure Centre will be closed immediately.
We propose to demolish the building and grant
planning permission for the land to be used for
the development of a new housing estate.

Submit your comments to:

**Ms Talia Albert
Head of Planning
Broxtown Council
3 Oak Lane
Broxtown
BR2 5NG**

WRITING TASK

Write a letter to Ms Talia Albert, Head of Planning, Broxtown Council, 3 Oak Lane, Broxtown, BR2 5NG.

In your letter you should:

• state whether you agree or disagree with the Council's proposals
• give detailed reasons to support your views
• state clearly what action you want the Council to take.

Remember to write in sentences and use Standard English.

(15 marks)

TASK F

INFORMATION

You read the following in the *Broxtown Local News*.

Life-Changing Moments

We've all had one – a moment when your life changes forever. It might be the day you left school, the day you started a new job or just a day when you did something absolutely amazing. Perhaps you took on a challenge for charity, or finally achieved a lifetime goal.

Why don't you get in touch and tell our readers about your life-changing moment? Whether your story is inspiring or simply amusing, we would like you to share your moment with our readers. The best moments will be published in the paper every Monday.

WRITING TASK

Write an article for the Broxtown Local News, describing your life-changing moment in detail.

In your article you should:

- say when your life-changing moment happened
- describe the occasion or experience that was life-changing
- explain what made it life-changing for you.

Remember to write in sentences and use Standard English.

(15 marks)

TASK G

INFORMATION

You read the following advertisement on a national newspaper's website.

Technology Detox

Do you spend hours on your mobile phone?
Do you sit for hours hunched over your laptop?
Is your life mainly spent online?

If so, research suggests that you could be damaging your health. Sitting and staring at a screen for long periods of time can lead to bad posture, back problems and poor eyesight. In addition, time spent on technology stops people from taking the exercise they need to keep their hearts, bones and lungs healthy.

Throughout the month of March we invite everyone to take up our Technology Detox challenge.
This challenge involves giving up technology for one hour every day and doing something that will benefit your health instead. You could go for a walk, or have an energetic workout at the gym.

You don't have to do this alone. Get all your friends involved to keep your motivation high!

WRITING TASK

You have decided to take up the challenge and would like your friend to join you.

Write an email to your friend, persuading them to take part in the Technology Detox challenge.

In your email you should:

- give detailed reasons why your friend should take part in the detox
- explain exactly what the detox involves
- describe the benefits of taking part.

Remember to write in sentences and use Standard English.

(15 marks)

TASK H

INFORMATION

You read this on a notice board at your school/college/workplace.

> **New Catering Grant!**
>
> We have been given £10,000 by the local authority to spend on our catering facilities.
>
> We are considering the following: re-decorating the canteen, buying new dining furniture, improving the lighting in the dining area, adding a patio area for outside dining, providing a new family-friendly dining area, or buying new equipment that will allow us to make and serve hot meals.
>
> We can only afford to do one of the above improvements. A survey has suggested that changes would be welcome, and we would like you to write a report suggesting which improvement would be most useful. Please explain why you think this improvement will benefit everyone.

WRITING TASK

Write a report for your school/college/workplace on how to spend the grant money. In your report you should:

- suggest which of the canteen areas needs improvement and why
- explain exactly what improvements should be made
- explain how the improvements will benefit everyone.

Remember to write in sentences and use Standard English.

(15 marks)

TASK 1

INFORMATION

You read the following in your local newspaper:

> **BURSTONE NATURE RESERVE**
> **OPENING MAY 2016**
>
> **Want to learn how to enjoy nature?**
> **Have fun while you learn!**
>
> Small animal zoo
> Children's adventure playground
> Nature trail – go with one of our experienced guides
> Bird-watching area
> Boating lake
> Café, restaurant & gift shop
> Climbing wall & high-ropes activity centre
>
> Free entry for first 100 visitors every day during opening week!
>
> **Open 10am–6pm**

WRITING TASK

You visited the Nature Reserve during the opening week. You decide to write a review of the Nature Reserve for the *Burstone Weekly*.

In your review you could:

- describe the attractions at the Nature Reserve
- state what you enjoyed about the Nature Reserve
- suggest who might enjoy the Nature Reserve and why.

Remember to write in sentences and use Standard English.

(15 marks)

TASK J

INFORMATION

You are on the committee for your local football club and receive the following email from the club secretary:

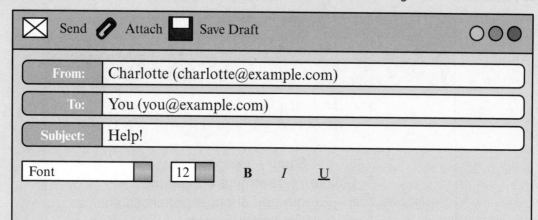

✉ Send   📎 Attach   💾 Save Draft   ○ ○ ●

From: Charlotte (charlotte@example.com)

To: You (you@example.com)

Subject: Help!

Font   12   **B**   *I*   U̲

Hi

Thanks for offering to help with our end-of-year committee meeting. The main matter we need to discuss is fundraising. I think we should put all our efforts into one fundraising event, perhaps a big formal ball held at a local hotel. If we charge for tickets and get local companies to donate raffle prizes and table decorations, we could raise a lot of money.

Not everybody agrees with me. Dan and Sally think we should spread our fundraising over the whole year and hold a lot of smaller events. Dan enters the local marathon and Sally does cake sales; they think events like these would be easier for the club to handle.

Can you put together a report about the two options so that we can discuss them at the meeting? We'll need an idea of the benefits/disadvantages of each.

Thanks
Charlotte

WRITING TASK

Write the report for the club committee meeting. In your report you should:

• explain the benefits of holding one large fundraising event
• explain the benefits of holding several smaller fundraising events
• suggest which you think would be best for the club.

Remember to write in sentences and use Standard English.

(15 marks)

Answers

READING

1. Your reading and writing tests

1 The main ideas

2 30 minutes

3 Check your work.

2. Online tools 1

1 Click the Time button.

2 Change the colour or font size.

3. Online tools 2

1 • Underlining words/phrases in questions

• Underlining words/phrases in reading texts

• Making a plan for answering writing tasks

2 Flag it and go back to it later by clicking the Review button.

4. Reading texts

1 • The main ideas

• The purpose

• The audience

• Key information

• Point of view, implicit meaning and bias

2 Yes, it can.

5. Skimming for details

1 Answers could include: heading, title, first sentence of each paragraph.

2 So you know what to look out for in the text.

6. Underlining

Three useful parts of the text should be underlined.

7. Types of question

1 Because you are not showing that you can use the text, so will not get marks for it.

2 Answers could include:

• what the question is asking you to do

• how long your answer needs to be

• what you need to include

• how many texts you need to use.

8. Reading test skills

To ensure you understand exactly what it is asking you to do, how many texts you need to use and how long or detailed your answer needs to be.

9. Analysing texts

1 • Audience

• Purpose

• Point of view

2 Implied meaning is the meaning behind the author's words.

10. Putting it into practice

Annotations should highlight key information in the text.

11. Identifying the main idea

For example:

• Text A: The main idea is that we all spend too much time using technology.

• Text B: The main idea is how to use technology wisely.

• Text C: The main idea is how technology can be good for children.

12. Texts that instruct

1 Any two of the following: manage, install, encourage, insulate, register, check, consider, fit, hang.

2 Answers could include:

• adults are more likely to own their home and think about insulation

• adults are more likely to be the ones paying the fuel bills.

13. Texts that inform

For example:

The main purpose of the text is to explain the negative effects of using technology. The title 'Are we all addicts?' shows this, and the word 'staggering' suggests that the amount of time young people spend using technology is shocking.

14. Texts that persuade

1 Paragraphs developed with lots of detail and figures suggest that the text is trying to persuade.

2 Words like 'vocabulary', 'absorption' and 'development' are quite complex and suggest the text is for parents.

3 Let children use technology but limit their child's onscreen time.

15. Language techniques 1

Answers could include:

• Formal style: 'Computer games … were found to be excellent preparation for writing and using tools' is written in a formal style to make the text seem authoritative.

• Descriptive language: Descriptive language like 'even the most techno-savvy child' makes technology sound exciting and positive.

• Emotive language: Words like 'moaning' and 'frustrating' suggest that the author understands how parents feel.

16. Language techniques 2

Answers could include:

• Counter-argument: 'There is no doubt that inappropriate content exists online, but…' shows that the author has thought about the dangers as well as the benefits of technology.

• Hyperbole: 'There is a whole world of development and learning at every child's fingertips' makes the positives of technology sound huge and almost endless.

• Direct address: Opening with 'Are you…' makes the reader sound and feel involved right from the start.

17. Fact and opinion

• Fact: 'my local museum has recently been renovated at a cost of £5.3 million'

• Fact: 'it sits on top of a hill surrounded by open fields'

• Opinion: 'the ideal spot for a mini wind farm'

18. Putting it into practice

Answers should resolve the mistakes highlighted in the sample answers.

19. Implicit meaning 1

Answers could include:

- 'prioritise': this suggests that the police are not currently taking any real action to help young homeless people.
- 'safe place': this suggests that homeless young people need to be looked after, not arrested.
- 'arresting them for begging': this suggests that the police regard homeless young people as criminals who should be put in prison rather than helped.

20. Implicit meaning 2

Answers could include:

- 'Putting on a jumper and turning the heating down could halve our winter bills.'
- 'We hear a lot about living in a throwaway society, but how many of us realise that the stuff we throw away includes fuel?'
- 'We will not achieve any significant savings until we learn to value the fuel we pay for.'

21. Point of view

1 B – the police are not doing enough to stop begging

2 It suggests the writer is concerned that not all beggars are honest and in need of the money.

22. Putting it into practice

1 B – too much technology can cause problems

2 For example:
- 'a bit of a dinosaur' - the writer thinks they are old-fashioned so they don't see technology as essential.
- a crafty look at my texts' – 'crafty' suggests that the writer feels guilty because technology is interrupting their work.

23. Using more than one text

1 Text A

2 Writing a longer answer and making it clear which text you are writing about.

24. Selecting quotations

Answers could include:

- The writer uses statistics, '75% of regular gamers had a longer attention span'.
- The writer uses expert evidence from a new study about gaming.
- The writer uses direct address, 'Are you dismayed'.

25. Using texts 1

1 Text I

2 The text is about a homeless charity.

3 For example: 'Homeless Haven offers a range of volunteering opportunities to choose from'.

26. Using texts 2

For example:

- Text G – 'donate to a shelter, soup kitchen or homeless charity, where your money will fund proper care'

- Text H – 'many young people are resorting to begging in order to feed themselves'
- Text I – 'money given to us in this way is vital'

27. Putting it into practice

11 Reason: Because it has tips about how to stay safe online.

Example: says you need to install special software to protect your computer files from being attacked and damaged by viruses

12 Text A: too much time on the computer can have a bad effect on your sleep patterns

Text C: sitting at the computer for too long stops you from getting out into the fresh air, which is good for your health

28. Summarising 1

D – Texts B and C both promote different reasons for using technology.

29. Summarising 2

For example:

- Text A – 'can disrupt sleep ... and make us less active'
- Text B – 'can lead to back pain and poor posture'

30. Writing a longer answer

Answers should use two or three examples and use appropriate signposting words. For example:

Both texts suggest that technology can help people develop skills. Text B says that 'there are loads of free apps' to help with skills including 'DIY' and 'baking'. Likewise Text C claims that children using technology can improve their communication skills. Both texts also suggest that technology can help with language. Text B suggests using technology to 'learn a new skill or language'. Similarly, Text C claims that 'active screen time also helps children develop language skills'.

31. Responding to a text 1

For example:

Text E gives advice about how to encourage teenagers to use less fuel.

32. Responding to a text 2

For example:

Also, social networking sites help children express themselves creatively [Text C].

33. Putting it into practice

1 For example: Also, young homeless people are often isolated and vulnerable. Many of them do not even have anywhere to go on Christmas Day.

2 The texts have different ideas about people who beg. For example, Text G says that people who beg spend the money on drugs and some of the people who beg work for criminal gangs. On the other hand, Text I says people who beg are just like the people on your street or at your college. Text I also says people who beg need help all year round.

34. Using a dictionary for reading

- competitive – as cheap as or cheaper than others available
- significantly – in a way that is easy to see or by a large amount

35. Avoiding common mistakes

Questions should have key words underlined.

4 It gives advice about how to save fuel, which is also a way to save money spent on fuel.

7 Answers could include:

- The writer uses 'we' to make the readers feel like the author is on their side.
- The writer uses expert opinion from the Chairman of the World Energy Trust to back up their opinions and make the text seem more reliable.
- They use a counter-argument: 'nobody is suggesting that hospitals start turning down the heating'. This shows they have thought about the other side of the problem.
- They give an example from their own experience – 'My children's school, for example'. This evidence backs up their opinions.
- The writer uses dramatic language like 'shocking', 'drastic' and 'irresponsible' to show how strongly they feel about fuel wastage.

13 C – Texts E and F both state that the environment is damaged by fuel waste.

36. Checking your work

Questions should have key words underlined.

9 Text A – 'means they spend half their lives staring at a screen'

Text C – 'Are you dismayed by the amount of time young people spend on their phones and tablets?'

11 Reason: Because it gives details about large organisations like schools and libraries and talks about how schools do not use green energy.

5 D – are not aware that fuel waste is a problem

WRITING

37. Writing test skills

1 Answers could include any three of the following:

- write clearly and concisely
- use details
- use suitable language for audience and purpose
- present information in a logical order
- structure your writing
- use correct grammar, spelling and punctuation.

2 When you don't know the audience and/or when the topic is serious.

38. Writing test questions

Write an article for your school/college/community newsletter.

In your article you may:

- describe the issue of litter in your local park
- explain why it is a problem
- state what you think should be done about it.

39. Letters, emails and reports

1 letter

2 report

3 email

40. Articles and reviews

Format	Structure
Letters	Date, addresses, Yours sincerely
Articles	Headings, sub-headings, paragraphs
Emails	Heading line, informal ending
Reviews	Engaging opening, detail of event, own opinion
Reports	Title, introduction, recommendation, conclusion

41. Speeches

Answers could include: an interesting opening sentence; direct address; paragraphs; different engaging language; facts and statistics; a meaningful ending.

For example: Why are uniforms important? Uniforms bring people together. They create a feeling of belonging, and they show that we are a proud to be part of our college community.

70% of students said that they would like to look smarter at college. As well as being smart, sensible and serious, uniforms have practical advantages. They ensure that students are comfortable and safe when working with potentially dangerous equipment in workshops.

You could even ask students to help design the uniform. This will encourage any students who aren't sure about uniforms that they will suit them too.

So, what are you waiting for? Uniforms bring people together!

42. Putting it into practice

For example:

Subject: Volunteer

Dear Sylvie,

I am writing to you to volunteer at the bring-and-buy sale.

I have a great idea for a new coffee stall. This would be a good way to encourage people to spend longer at the sale and hopefully spend more money.

I work in a café at weekends, so know how to make a range of hot and cold drinks. I have always been interested in charity work. At school my friends and I ran a cake stall, and raised hundreds of pounds towards a new computer suite.

Regards,

Jessica Gantry

43. Inform, explain, describe, review

1 The main idea of the article.

2 For example:

Fact – wildlife can be seriously harmed by plastic containers left as litter; lots of litter on the floor can be a hazard that could cause people to trip and fall

Statistic – only 20% of people ever leave litter; 70% of litter is fast-food containers

3 For example:

Use vivid descriptive language that appeals to the senses, conveying the ugliness and smell of litter, and simple, direct command verbs encouraging the reader to take action.

44. Argue and persuade

1 Answers could include:

- Local people use the park on a regular basis
- It allows people to exercise for free

- People without gardens have nowhere else to go to enjoy the summer
- It helps children learn about nature
- It provides food and shelter for local wildlife
- Community groups base their activities there.

2 For example:

You may think that the park is only used by teenagers messing around, but it also helps young children learn about nature.

45. Audience

- Task F: general audience, from Broxton, mostly adults
- Task G: specific audience, someone you know well, can be informal
- Task H: college, large audience, could include staff as well as students so formal

46. Formal writing

For example:

The Leisure Centre's facilities are a vital part of the battle to keep people fit and healthy. Many local residents cannot afford the high monthly fees charged by private fitness clubs so they rely on council-operated centres for their weekly exercise sessions.

47. Informal writing

For example:

Do you have any idea how much damage you're doing to your neck and back when you're slumped in front of that TV? Hunching for hours over a laptop playing games, surfing the net, or chatting with your mates could mean you'll be old before your time.

48. Putting it into practice

For example:

The Menace of Litter

Public areas ruined

Broxtown Park is beautiful. It boasts a well-tended bowls green, six tennis courts and a welcoming café serving tasty snacks and hot drinks. It used to be a lovely area for a stroll, or a calm place to sit and rest in the middle of a busy day. Unfortunately, it is now ruined by a carpet of litter.

Answers should continue with appropriate sub-headings, style and content.

49. Planning

Audience, purpose and format should be underlined. Relevant information in the task should also be underlined. The plan should include:

- subject heading
- ideas for each task bullet point
- detail from the task information.

50. Using detail

Audience, purpose and format should be underlined. Relevant information in the task should also be underlined. The plan should include:

- title and sub-headings
- ideas for each task bullet point
- detail from the task information
- appropriate features, such as facts and statistics.

51. Paragraphs

1 For example:

1 playground damage, swings broken, children disappointed

2 no sign about dangers, muddy walkways, litter on paths

3 large menu, long wait for hot food, no ice cream

2 For example:

All my children wanted to do was visit the adventure playground. They chatted endlessly about the zip wire, the tyre swing and the obstacle course. However, they nearly cried when we found broken swings, a damaged zip wire and so much mud that it was impossible to see any of the obstacles.

52. Point-Evidence-Explain

For example:

Another proposal is to hold several smaller fundraising events throughout the year. For example, Dan wants to raise sponsorship by running a marathon, Sally wants to hold regular cake sales and John thinks we could run a monthly produce stall at the local market. A range of events would ensure all members feel involved in the life of the club.

53. Linking ideas

For example:

Firstly, you know you don't do enough exercise. For example, you spend at least four hours of every day playing video games. Also you take the bus to work, even though it is less than a mile! As a result, you're at risk of heart disease and obesity.

54. Putting it into practice

Answers should use new paragraphs for each idea, a range of adverbials to link ideas and an appropriate counter-argument.

55. Vocabulary

For example:

The Council must **appreciate** the effect the closure will have on the **well-being** of the local community. Closing the Leisure Centre will be an **absolute calamity** for everybody, but it will be particularly **disastrous** for those who use it for health reasons.

56. Language techniques 1

For example:

- Rhetorical question – Did the café save the day?
- Direct address – You'll find the café makes the trip worthwhile.
- Lists – Visiting the café made us feel a little better as we found a delicious variety of sandwiches, jacket potato fillings, cakes and ice cream flavours.
- Repetition – We found broken swings, a broken zip wire and even a broken seat in the playground area.

57. Language techniques 2

For example:

- Alliteration – The trip was scary so I needed some serious safety equipment.
- Personification – Sunshine blinked at me from the calm blue water.
- Simile – The café looked like an oasis of calm in the middle of the busy street.
- Metaphor – The island was a rare and precious jewel in the ocean.

58. Putting it into practice

Paragraphs should use language that is suitable for audience, format and purpose and should include:

- emotive language for impact
- alternatives to the words 'climbing' and 'really'.

59. Sentences

For example:

My first day at school. I was so scared when I looked up at the door I could hear my knees knocking. Loads of people rushed past me while I stood there, rooted to the spot.

60. Sentence variety

For example:

Above me loomed the biggest hill I had ever seen. Holding on tightly to the map I had been given by the guide, I set off. Slow and steady was the only way to tackle this type of journey.

61. Writing about the present and future

1 I ~~wakes~~/wake up every day at 6am for work.
2 Ben ~~are going~~/is going to take his mother to the nature reserve next year.
3 They will arrive/~~arrives~~ at 5pm.
4 I love my new alarm clock; it wakes/~~wake~~ me up very gently.

62. Writing about the past

We ~~have~~/had a fantastic day at Burstone Nature Reserve! We followed/~~follows~~ the nature trail for miles until we were/~~was~~ tired out. Ben and I ~~see~~/saw lots of different birds. Ben ~~laughs~~/laughed as I ~~copyed~~/copied the bird noises on the way round.

63. Putting it into practice

First paragraph should have sentences joined using linking words and the tense corrected.

Second paragraph example:

Many of my skills make me suitable for volunteering. For example, I am an excellent cook and have worked as a part-time chef in a local restaurant. Before university I worked as an activity organiser on a camping site, which has given me valuable experience of entertaining children of all ages. Also, I love working with people and feel I am very friendly and approachable.

64. Full stops and capital letters

1 Do you want your child hurt by these loose tiles?
2 Jane Smith suggested I send my complaint to you.
3 Don't hold a lit firework!

65. Commas

1 I really wanted a hot meal, but the Bistro is closed on Mondays.
2 A new hot food area, which need not be too costly, would benefit all employees.
3 When the hot food area has been fitted, employees will not need to leave the building at lunchtime.
4 We could consider adding a pizza oven, a jacket potato oven, a salad bar and a coffee machine.

66. Apostrophes and inverted commas

1 Barbara's Bistro is simply the best in town.
2 It's best to visit the Nature Reserve in the summer.
3 When I visited the Reserve I took the book '101 British Birds' with me.
4 "This restaurant's burgers are the biggest in town," another diner assured me.

67. Spelling tips

1 Every paying visitor to the Nature Reserve receives a receipt.
2 My mother told me to visit the Nature Reserve as it has lovely views.
3 When I get to the house, I could surprise my mother.

68. Common spelling errors 1

1 The boots are ~~two~~/~~to~~/too muddy to go in the car.
2 You are/~~our~~ lucky to be going on holiday.
3 Students should take their/~~they're~~/~~there~~ books to each lesson.
4 The plane takes off/~~of~~ in an hour.
5 ~~Your~~/You're going to love the film.

69. Common spelling errors 2

1 With my new pen, I can ~~right~~/write in the ~~write~~/right style.
2 I ~~now~~/know I ~~should of~~/should have looked where I was going.
3 I could have/~~could of~~ bought/~~brought~~ it cheaper at another shop.
4 The new mobile I ~~brought~~/bought from Estrick Electronics is faulty.

70. Common spelling errors 3

Have you practised the tricky spellings?

71. Plurals

1 For the ~~partys~~/parties we need fourteen ~~loafs~~/loaves of bread.
2 All the ~~torchs~~/torches need new batteries/~~batterys~~.
3 A family ticket covers two adults and up to three ~~childs~~/children on all ~~buss~~/buses.
4 Men/~~Mans~~ are just as clever as ~~womans~~/women.

72. Checking your work

Have you checked the plans and answers that you have written already for mistakes?

73. Putting it into practice

Answer should correct all 12 spelling mistakes, the four punctuation mistakes and one style error, then add more detail about the disadvantages of holding a ball.

74. Putting it into practice (Example answer)

Answer should have the mistakes corrected and extra detail added.

75. Putting it into practice (Example answer)

Answer should have the spelling mistakes identified and corrected. The second and third paragraphs should be rewritten with linked sentences, interesting vocabulary and extra detail.

Notes

Notes

Published by Pearson Education Limited, 80 Strand, London, WC2R 0RL.

www.pearsonschoolsandfecolleges.co.uk

Copies of official specifications for all Edexcel qualifications may be found on the website: www.edexcel.com

Text © Pearson Education Limited 2017
Edited, typeset and produced by Elektra Media Ltd
Original illustrations © Pearson Education Limited 2017
Illustrated by Elektra Media Ltd
Cover illustration by Miriam Sturdee

The right of Julie Hughes to be identified as author of this work has been asserted by her in accordance with the Copyright, Designs and Patents Act 1988.

First published 2017

20 19 18 17
10 9 8 7 6 5 4 3 2 1

British Library Cataloguing in Publication Data
A catalogue record for this book is available from the British Library

ISBN 978 1 292 14581 5

Printed in Slovakia by Neografia

A note from the publisher
In order to ensure that this resource offers high-quality support for the associated Pearson qualification, it has been through a review process by the awarding body. This process confirms that this resource fully covers the teaching and learning content of the specification or part of a specification at which it is aimed. It also confirms that it demonstrates an appropriate balance between the development of subject skills, knowledge and understanding, in addition to preparation for assessment.

Endorsement does not cover any guidance on assessment activities or processes (e.g. practice questions or advice on how to answer assessment questions), included in the resource nor does it prescribe any particular approach to the teaching or delivery of a related course.

While the publishers have made every attempt to ensure that advice on the qualification and its assessment is accurate, the official specification and associated assessment guidance materials are the only authoritative source of information and should always be referred to for definitive guidance.

Pearson examiners have not contributed to any sections in this resource relevant to examination papers for which they have responsibility.

Examiners will not use endorsed resources as a source of material for any assessment set by Pearson. Endorsement of a resource does not mean that the resource is required to achieve this Pearson qualification, nor does it mean that it is the only suitable material available to support the qualification, and any resource lists produced by the awarding body shall include this and other appropriate resources.